BRIDLINGTON

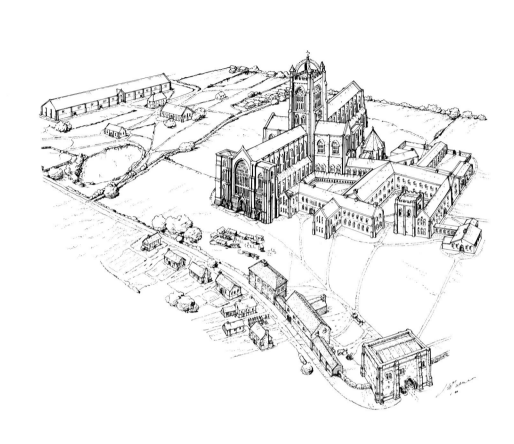

BRIDLINGTON

An Introduction to its History and Buildings

David and Susan Neave

First published in 2000 by
Smith Settle Ltd
Ilkley Road
Otley
West Yorkshire
LS21 3JP

ISBN Paperback   1 85825 137 0
         Hardback   1 85825 138 9

Frontispiece: The Augustinian Priory of Bridlington from the west as
it may have been in 1537. A conjectural reconstruction by Les Turner
based on the work of John Earnshaw.

Set in Monotype Plantin and Gill.

Designed, printed and bound by
SMITH SETTLE
Ilkley Road, Otley, West Yorkshire LS21 3JP

Contents

The Lords Feoffees and Assistants of the Manor of Bridlington

The Lords Feoffees and Assistants of the Manor of Bridlington, Thursday 3 February 2000. (Left to right.) Front row, seated. Lords — Dr T.R. Wilson, G.Q. Gray, B.H. Rodgers, Deputy Chief Lord N.W. Newby, Chief Lord B.F.H. Gray, Senior Lord C.Wilson, B.R. Langton, M.A. Horrox, H.D. Whitehead. Rear, standing: Assistants — H.T. Wood, J.M. Bapty, Dr A.J.S. Watson, D. Stevenson, R.C. Witty, R.H. Sharpe, A.C. Boughton, D.E. Robson, A.G. Newby, I.A. Thompson, D.P. Mooney.

In 1630 the Manor of Bridlington was purchased by thirteen townsmen acting on behalf of themselves and the rest of the inhabitants. Six years later, on 6 May 1636, the purchasers entered into an agreement with the 187 tenants and free-holders of the manor. Under the agreement, known as the Great Town Deed, the thirteen purchasers were constituted as Feoffees* to act as trustees, on behalf of all the townspeople, with the help of twelve Assistants.

At the beginning of the 21ˢᵗ century the Lords Feoffees and Assistants of the Manor of Bridlington, as they are officially known, are an active and influential body in the town. The income of the Lords Feoffees, who are a registered charity, is 'employed for the public use and benefit of Bridlington'.

Each year one of the Lords Feoffees is chosen as Chief Lord and during his year of office he takes a lease of the manor from the other Lords in trust. When the Lords Feoffees are reduced to six the number is made up to thirteen from the Assistants and an election is held to fill the vacancies amongst the latter. Lords and Assistants must be owners of freehold property in the manor at the time of election and the right to vote for the Assistants is also restricted to freeholders of the manor.

*A feoffee is someone who holds land in trust for charitable or other public purposes.

Preface

Bright, Breezy, Bracing. To many people Bridlington is just a place for a holiday or an outing, a busy seaside resort on the Yorkshire coast with wonderful sandy beaches, a fascinating harbour and plenty of amusements. But Bridlington is so much more as this introduction to its history shows; a history echoed in its streets and buildings — the great medieval Priory church, the long curving High Street with its splendid 17th-century merchants' houses, the 19th-century harbour and the terraces, villas and other reminders of the late Victorian and Edwardian resort.

The three Bs. The arms of the manor of Bridlington, 1663. They were formerly used as the arms of the Augustinian Priory of St Mary, Bridlington.

This book, the initial publication resulting from a major research project on the history of Bridlington commissioned by the Lords Feoffees and Assistants of the Manor of Bridlington, is to be followed later this year by a much more substantial history of the market town, port and resort.

Although having its foundations in the work of three 19th-century local historians, John Thompson, Marmaduke Prickett and John Browne, and drawing heavily on more recent published work by Canon J.S.Purvis, Keith Allison, Edward Ingram and others listed in the sources and acknowledgements, the full study is the result of extensive original research. A great wealth of documentary material has been examined in the East Riding Archive Office, Beverley, the Borthwick Institute of Historical Research at the University of York, the University of Hull Archives, the Public Record Office, Kew and from the Lords Feoffees' Town Chest at the Bayle. The splendid collection of printed material, including local newspapers, in the Local Studies Library at Bridlington, has been an invaluable resource.

As with all research the more we have explored the sources the more we have become aware that the task can never be completed. Much remains to be done by present and future historians of Bridlington. Many important topics deserve further study and we hope this will inspire others to fill the gaps. In particular we would like to encourage more research on the history of the town in the last fifty years and the contemporary recording of life in Bridlington in the 21st century. A vital ingredient of this research will be oral history to which all can contribute.

David and Susan Neave
University of Hull
February 2000

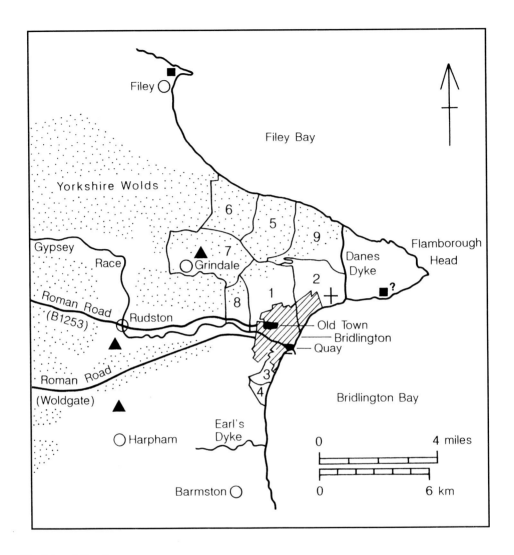

Parish of Bridlington —
location and historical setting:

☒ built-up area

▲ site of Roman villa

■ site of Roman signal station

✚ Sewerby Anglian cemetery

Parish of Bridlington — townships:

1. Bridlington; 2. Sewerby
and Marton; 3. Hilderthorpe;
4. Wilsthorpe (part); 5. Buckton;

Origins

The East Yorkshire town of Bridlington is really two settlements, generally known as the Old Town and the Quay. They were physically separate until the later 19th century.

The Quay is situated at the point where the Gypsey Race, a small and erratic stream that runs through the northern Wolds, enters Bridlington Bay. The mouth of the Gypsey Race, sheltered from the north by the Flamborough peninsula, forms a natural harbour and it is likely that there has been a landing place here from prehistoric times. The Old Town, a mile inland, was probably settled in the Anglo-Saxon period. During the middle ages it developed as an agricultural and marketing community in the shadow of a wealthy and powerful monastery.

The ancient ecclesiastical parish of Bridlington covered some 14,400 acres (5828 ha.) and included the nine townships of Buckton, Easton, Grindale, Hilderthorpe, Marton, Sewerby, Speeton, Wilsthorpe and Bempton (which became an independent parish in 1441) and part of Auburn. This book is concerned only with the manor and township of Bridlington, which covered 2,519 acres (1085 ha.) in 1851, and those parts of Bessingby, Hilderthorpe and Sewerby into which the urban area spread in the late 19th and 20th centuries (see plan on p.82).

Romans and Anglo-Saxons

There is strong evidence to suggest that there was a port at the mouth of the Gypsey Race in the Roman period, for Bridlington Bay has been identified with the 'Safehaven Bay' recorded by the 2nd-century geographer Ptolemy. The name 'Castleburn', sometimes used in the middle ages for the Quay, may also indicate a Roman settlement. Two possible Roman roads lead to Bridlington from the west; one along the line of the present Woldgate, through Kilham, and the other along the valley of the Gypsey Race, through Rudston. They would have been routeways to the sea from the important Roman centres of York and Malton.

Around Bridlington there is a cluster of Roman villa sites at Rudston, Harpham and Grindale, and some earthworks at Sewerby, said to be Roman, disappeared with a cliff fall at the

Danes Dyke from the north. *(Cambridge University Collection of Air Photographs: copyright reserved)* This two-and-a-half mile (4 km.) long earthwork formed the eastern boundary of the ancient parish of Bridlington.

Coin of the Emperor Hadrian. Some 40 Roman coins have been collected on the sands of Bridlington Bay.

A buckle from the Anglian cemetery at Sewerby excavated in 1959 and 1974. (*Department of Archaeology, University of York*) Over 50 graves were uncovered from the late 5th to 7th century. One had the skeletons of two women, one of whom had been buried alive.

beginning of the 20th century. Any vestige of a Roman port or other settlement at Bridlington Quay would have been long destroyed by coastal erosion. The coastline in the Roman period would have been between one and two kilometres further east.

In the late 4th century the threat of attacks from the sea led the Romans to build a series of fortified signal stations along the Yorkshire coast, and it is thought that one may have stood to the northeast of Bridlington, on Flamborough Head. The nearby Danes Dyke must also have been built as a defence, but by whom? Over the last two centuries antiquarians, historians and archaeologists have put forward a host of theories. For some this massive earthwork is undoubtedly of the Bronze Age (up to 3000 years ago), others date it to the Iron Age (around 2000 years ago) but more recently opinion has swayed in favour of the Anglo-Saxon period (around 1300 years ago). All seem to agree that it was not built by the Danes!

If Anglo-Saxon the earthwork would be associated with the important Anglian presence in the area from the late 5th century that has left its mark in the major pagan cemetery at Sewerby. Many local place names have the Danish endings *-by* meaning farm or estate and *-thorpe* meaning hamlet, suggesting some settlement in the area by the Vikings who established a kingdom at York in 866. The name Bridlington, however, is Anglian in origin, derived from two Anglo-Saxon words, the personal name *Berhtel* and *ingtun* meaning farmstead. The recorded history of Bridlington, as for almost all settlements in the East Riding, begins with the Domesday Book of 1086, in which it is referred to as *Bretlinton*.

[Domesday Book manuscript text reproduction]

The entry in Domesday Book recording William the Conqueror's manor of *Bretlinton* in 1086.

Domesday Book

Domesday Book records that on the eve of the Norman invasion the land at Bridlington was held by three Anglo-Scandinavians, Morcar with nine carucates*, Torchil with five carucates and Carle with four. Of these the most powerful was Morcar, Earl of Northumberland, who in 1068 rebelled unsuccessfully against King William and forfeited his lands including the manor of Bridlington.

In 1086 the king had the former lands of both Morcar and Carle and his half-brother Robert, Count of Mortain, held Torchil's manor. The last was described as 'all waste' and the king's manor, which had been worth £32 in 1066, was only valued at 8s (40p). Although such a marked decline, evident throughout Yorkshire, cannot necessarily be attributed to the 'harrying of the North' of 1069 when William 'ravaged and laid waste the whole shire' (*Anglo-Saxon Chronicle*), it clearly indicates that the settlements were in decay.

A church is recorded at Bridlington in 1086 and four burgesses who paid rent. The reference to burgesses (inhabitants of a borough) usually suggests the existence of a town but in this case it is thought that they may have been freemen brought in by the king to revive the fortunes of a strategically important settlement. The importance lay in the presence of the port although this is not mentioned in Domesday Book.

Bridlington was the centre of a major royal estate with two berewicks*, Hilderthorpe and Wilsthorpe and a soke* comprising lands in thirteen settlements including Bessingby, Boynton, Buckton, Easton, Grindale, Marton, Sewerby and Speeton as well as the more distant villages of Ganton, Staxton and Willerby. Bridlington lay in the hundred* of Huntou. The name of this division, later part of the wapentake* of Dickering, is preserved in the field and farm name, Huntow, north of the town.

*Glossary

Carucate: A unit of taxation rather than a measurement of land. It is derived from the amount of land a team of eight oxen could plough in a year. About 120 acres (48.5 ha.)

Berewick: A dependent settlement within a manor.

Soke: A dependent free territory.

Hundred: An administrative, military and judicial subdivision replaced in the East Riding in the 12th century by the larger *Wapentake*.

The Gant family and the founding of Bridlington Priory

Not long after the compilation of Domesday Book the royal manor of Bridlington was granted to the powerful Norman baron, Gilbert de Gant, who died c. 1095. Gant, from Flanders, had come to England with King William. He helped suppress the risings in the north and received large estates in Lincolnshire, Nottinghamshire and Yorkshire. His principal Yorkshire manor was at Hunmanby.

Around 1113 Gilbert's son, Walter de Gant, 'at the request and with the consent' of Henry I, established a priory of regular canons under the Rule of St Augustine at Bridlington, the first Augustinian house in the north of England. Houses of regular canons, that is clergy living together following the monastic life, had become particularly popular on the continent in the later 11th century. The Augustinian order, which reached England around 1095 with the founding of a priory at Colchester, was particularly favoured by King Henry I and his wife Matilda. During his reign (1100-35) some 40 English priories were established and the king took a personal interest in the founding of Bridlington, granting the canons lands at Easton and Hilderthorpe.

The major endowments to the priory on its foundation came from Walter de Gant and his tenants. Walter granted the canons his property at Bridlington, including the church and mills, as well as churches in the North Riding, Lincolnshire and Derbyshire.

On Walter's death around 1139 he was succeeded by his son Gilbert de Gant who had been born and raised at Bridlington Priory. During the unrest of King Stephen's reign Gilbert quarrelled with his powerful neighbour William of Aumale, Lord of Holderness. Aumale attacked Bridlington Priory, turned out the canons and fortified the monastic buildings as a 'castle'. This incident was short-lived and the priory was soon afterwards restored to the canons who later received grants of land and other rights from Aumale.

Throughout the 12th century and 13th century Bridlington Priory continued to receive substantial benefactions. The patronage of the Gant family was particularly important. Gilbert de Gant, who expressed a wish to enter the priory himself

A 12th-century grave slab of Tournai marble in the Priory church, Bridlington. Almost certainly from the grave of Gilbert de Gant (died 1156) who asked to be buried in the Priory. (*Prickett*)

in his old age, granted the canons lands in Bessingby, Speeton, Burton Fleming and Hunmanby and the services of tenants.

The priory lands and possessions

The many grants of land, rights and churches made Bridlington Priory one of the wealthiest and most powerful monasteries in Yorkshire by the later middle ages. In 1535 it had twice the wealth of the monasteries of Meaux, Kirkham and Rievaulx, but only half the wealth of Fountains.

The greater part of the priory land was in East Yorkshire, where in addition to Bridlington the canons had important holdings in Burton Fleming, Fraisthorpe, Bessingby, Buckton, Sewerby, Marton, Skirlington, Speeton, Little Kelk, Acklam, Staxton and Willerby. They also had land in Lincolnshire and large tracts in the North and West Ridings; in Swaledale, based on Grinton, and at Blubberhouses, between Harrogate and Skipton. As well as land the priory derived a substantial income, through tithes, by its possession of sixteen churches and around twelve chapelries. These included, locally, the churches at Scarborough, Flamborough, Filey, Ganton, Atwick, Carnaby and Boynton with others in Lincolnshire, Derbyshire and Warwickshire.

Records of the farming of the estate at Burton Fleming in the 14th century reveal an emphasis on arable farming with barley as the principal crop. Elsewhere on the Yorkshire Wolds and in Lincolnshire the canons had extensive sheep pastures. The priory was a leading wool producer, no doubt exporting some through the port of Bridlington, their ownership of which was confirmed by King Stephen along with 'all kinds of wreck of the sea … within the Dykes called Earl Dyke and Flaynburg Dyke (Danes Dyke)'. Priory wool was also exported from Filey and Kingston-upon-Hull, via the river Hull.

The produce of the more local estates, including the tithes, would be brought into Bridlington and gathered into the great priory barn which stood to the north of the church. Corn would be ground at the priory's four windmills and two water mills in Bridlington and sold with other produce at the weekly market and annual fairs.

In 1200 the prior and convent were granted the right to hold a market weekly (on Saturday) and an annual fair on 14-15 August (the eve and feast

Double capitals of c. 1150-75 from reconstructed cloister arcade in Bridlington Priory Church. *(East Riding of Yorkshire Council)*

Part of a page from the 14th-century cartulary of Bridlington Priory relating to lands at Buckton *(reproduced by permission of the British Library - ADD.MS 40008 F38).*

Head of a king from a
13th-century capital in the North
Porch of Bridlington Priory.

The nave of Bridlington Priory
church looking west, c. 1900.
(Martin Craven)

of the assumption of the Blessed Virgin Mary).
Three more fairs were granted in 1446 to be held
annually on 7-9 September (the vigil, feast and
morrow of the nativity of the Blessed Virgin Mary),
10 October (the feast of St John of Bridlington)
and 10-12 May (the vigil, feast and morrow of the
translation of St John of Bridlington).

The priory buildings

The aisled nave of the priory church and the
gateway, known as the Bayle, are all that survive of
the great complex of buildings that made up the
medieval priory. The rest of the buildings were
cleared away soon after the dissolution in 1537.
The layout of the priory can be reconstructed
from a survey made of the greater part of the
monastic buildings at the dissolution and from
records of chance finds in the churchyard and limited archaeological investigations.

The church

The earliest mention of a church at Bridlington
is in 1086. It can be assumed that building formed
the nucleus of the priory on its foundation in 1113
and that the Priory church stands on its site.
There is nothing in the present building, except
the sections of reconstructed cloister arcade of
c. 1150-75 and certain stonework, that date from
before the 13th century when the bulk of the
present church was built. Work commenced soon
after 1200 with the lower part of the north-west
tower, followed by the north side of the church
including the splendid north porch of around
1240-50. The south side of the church was built
c.1260-1300 although the three easternmost bays
were reconstructed in the early 15th century, possibly as the first phase of the rebuilding of the west
end, a project that was never completed. The tops
of the present west towers are a result of Sir
George Gilbert Scott's Victorian restoration.

Although impressive the present building was
only part of the medieval church. It is 185 feet
(56 m.) long, but the church, when complete, was
some 333 feet (100 m.) long, the same as Beverley
Minster. The dissolution survey recorded that the
tall central tower contained seven bells but it was
'dangerously in decay'. To the east of the tower
stood the choir which had been fitted out in the
early 16th century with new stalls 'after the right

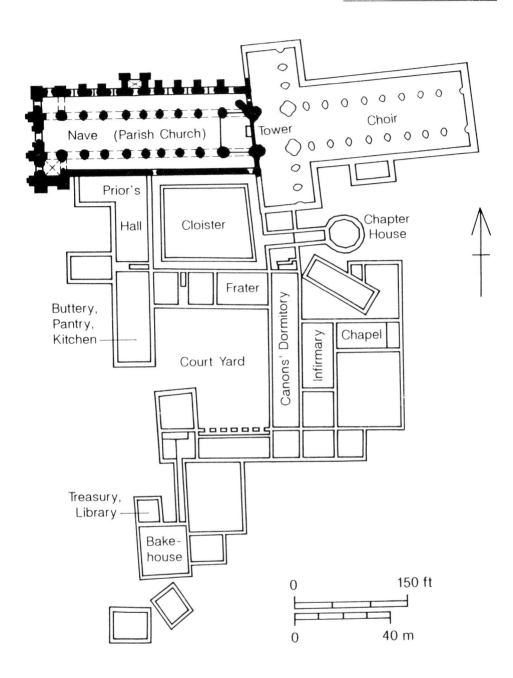

Conjectural plan of Bridlington Priory in 1537, redrawn by Mike Frankland, based on the work of John Earnshaw.

goodly fashion'. The reredos at the back of the high altar was covered in statues. It was 'of a great height ... excellently well wrought and ... well gilded'.

Between the high altar and the east window was the shrine of St John of Bridlington (see p. 11). Underneath the shrine were five chapels with altars and small alabaster tables and images.

The conventual buildings

On the south side of the nave was the cloister that excavations have shown was not square. The main monastic buildings were arranged around the cloister. On the west side was the prior's lodgings containing a large hall and chambers and at the south end of the hall were the buttery, pantry, and prior's kitchen. The chapter house, where the canons would meet daily to transact business, was on the east side of the cloister. Also on this side was the canons' dormitory reached by twenty stone steps. Further east was the infirmary.

To the south of the main priory buildings were a bakehouse and brewhouse which old men claimed had been 'sometime a nunnery'. Rather than a nunnery this was probably the Hospital of St Mary the Virgin that existed from around 1130 until at least the mid-14th century.

North of the priory church, across the present Sewerby Road, was the 'barn yard' with various farm buildings including the great barn which was 117 yards (107 m.) long and 27 yards (25 m.) wide. South of the barn were a granary, malthouse and kiln and nearby 'a pretty house with a chamber where the harvest men did always dine'.

The Priory church from the south west, 1831. *(Prickett)* The place where the cloister and prior's lodgings were attached to the church can be clearly seen at the south side of the nave.

Daily life and learning

A good account of the daily life of the canons of Bridlington Priory in its early days is provided by a commentary on the Rule of St Augustine, in the form of a dialogue between the master and a pupil, written by the third prior, Robert of Bridlington or Robert the Scribe, in the mid-12th century. The daily pattern was determined by attendance at seven services in the choir. The day began at dawn with Matins and Prime, followed by Terce at 9 a.m., Sext at noon, None at 3 p.m., Vespers at sundown, and Compline at 9 p.m. The canons then retired to bed for two and a half hours before Vigils at midnight after which they could sleep until dawn. There were only two meals a day, dinner after Terce and supper sometime after None.

The canons, when not praying, eating or sleeping undertook tasks apportioned by the prior. Some worked in the gardens, growing vegetables and herbs; or in the fields, ploughing, sowing and reaping. Others mended clothes, made baskets and nets and wove rush mats. Some would practice their singing or reading parts of the services;

The Augustinian Hugh of St Victor at Paris teaching a group of canons. *(By permission of the Bodleian Library, University of Oxford – MS.Laud. Misc.409, fol.3v)* A manuscript painting executed at St Albans in the later 12th century. Achard, a former canon of Bridlington, became abbot of St Victor in 1165 and amongst the canons there in the late 12th century was Robert of Flamborough.

others would be teaching, or working as scribes in the scriptorium.

Bridlington Priory had a reputation as a centre for learning. In addition to Robert the Scribe and St John of Bridlington (see below), the chroniclers Peter de Langtoft and the unknown author of *Gesta Edwardi de Carnavon* (a life of King Edward II) and the alchemist George Ripley were canons of Bridlington. Ripley, who died in 1490, was one of the most important of English alchemists. He travelled in France, Germany and Italy and lived for some time in Rome. He later returned to Bridlington where he pursued the art of alchemy, that is the transformation of baser metals

A page from a late 14th-century breviary of Bridlington Priory. *(Lords Feoffees)*

into gold, and produced many works in verse and the *Compound of Alchemy*.

The medieval town and port

Very little is known about the town of Bridlington in the middle ages. Chiefly an agricultural community, it was small and dominated by the priory. In tax lists before the late 14th century it is ranked below Kilham and its urban status is doubtful. The market and annual fairs, and the harbour, clearly encouraged trade and there are incidental references to a range of occupations including merchants, tanners, tailors, weavers, smiths, stonemasons, shoemakers, brewers and bakers.

There is little information on the trade of the port at Castleburn (the Quay). The prior owned ships and there are occasional mentions of vessels from the Low Countries and the Baltic being driven ashore in the bay. There was some foreign trade, for example in 1403 a Bridlington ship the *St John* was loaded with wine at Bordeaux. However in the late middle ages the trade was largely coastal, exporting corn to, and importing coal and salt from, the north-east. Some fishing also took place.

Court records suggest that medieval Bridlington was a far from peaceable place and during the Anglo-Scottish wars of the late 13th and early 14th centuries the town was vulnerable to attack from sea and land. In autumn 1322 Robert the Bruce invaded England and on 14 October the Scots forces converged on Edward II and the English army at Byland Abbey. Edward fled to Pickering then on to Bridlington Priory where he spent the night before going to his manor house at Burstwick. One of the canons was sent to Malton to treat with the Scots whilst the priory treasure was sent into Lincolnshire. A force of Scots did advance to Bridlington where nine horsemen and eighteen horses were given accommodation in the priory.

St John of Bridlington

John de Thweng (or Thwing) was born at the village of Thwing, nine miles west of Bridlington, in about 1320. After having studied for two years at Oxford he entered Bridlington Priory as a canon before he was twenty. He held the offices of sacrist, master of the novices, cellarer, sub-prior

St John of Bridlington from a 15th-century Book of Hours of the Blessed Virgin Mary. (*By permission of the British Library – MS Royal 2A XVIII F7V*)

The shrine of St John of Bridlington from a damaged manuscript in the British Library. *(Prickett)* In 1405 the relics of St John were placed in a splendid new shrine by the Archbishop of York and the Bishops of Lincoln and Carlisle. The shrine, which was situated between the high altar and the east window, was in a 'fair' chapel, raised up with a stairway on either side 'for to go and come by'.

and finally prior in 1363. Prior John became renowned for his humility, learning and holiness. An active monastic reformer he is said to have insisted on a rule of simplicity, equality, abstinence and prayer. He despised all worldly pomp. Rather than use the 'large and fair chamber' set aside for the prior with all its fine furnishings and adornments he slept every night in a cell in the common dormitory. His bedding and clothing were cheap and coarse but decent.

During his lifetime, as well as his great care of the poor, he is credited with carrying out many miracles including walking on the sea to rescue sailors caught in a storm, turning water into wine, raising the dead, multiplying corn, curing the sick and fortelling the hour of his death. After his death in 1379 the miracles multiplied; at least five people were said to have been restored to life by his intervention, two women had their sight restored and many others were cured of fevers and other sicknesses. Pilgrimages began to be made to Prior John's tomb in the Priory church and after enquiries carried out for the Archbishop of York in 1386 and the Pope in 1391 he was canonised as St John of Bridlington on 24 September 1401. He was the last Englishman to be made a saint before the Reformation. The feast day of St John was decreed to be 10 October.

There were many bequests to the shrine of St John of Bridlington who was ranked high amongst the English saints. In the early 15th century Richard Beauchamp, Earl of Warwick left to the shrine

St John of Bridlington from a 15th-century stained glass window in the vestry of St Matthew's Church, Morley, Derbyshire, redrawn by J.S. Purvis.

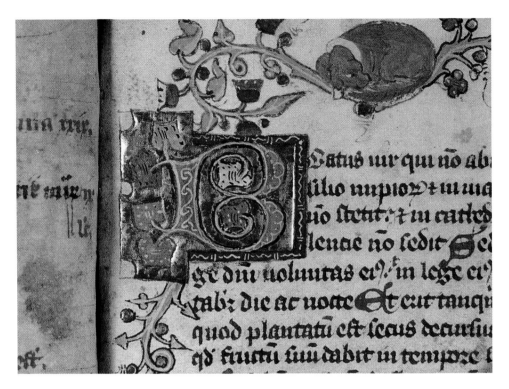

Illuminated letters from a late 14th-century breviary of Bridlington Priory. This manuscript service book, containing psalms, hymns and lessons with charming illuminated letters and marginal decorations, is displayed in the Bayle Museum. *(Lords Feoffees)*

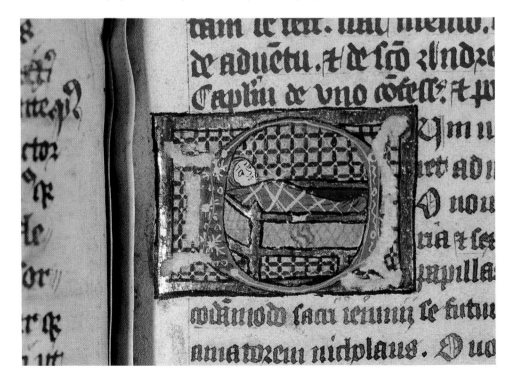

The Bayle in the mid-19th century. *(Lords Feoffees)* In 1388 King Richard II, out of regard for the late prior John, granted the prior and convent a licence to enclose and fortify the priory. The priory gateway, the Bayle, dates from this time. The painting shows a fair or cattle market being held on Church Green.

'his image in pure gold weighing twenty pounds' and the rector of Clayworth, Nottinghamshire, left 'a gilded belt once belonging to my lord the Archbishop together with a joint of the finger of St John of Brydlyngton'. Local donors included Richard Barnard of Speeton who left his silver belt to be hung round the shrine of St John and the wealthy Bridlington merchant Robert Coke who left a pair of silver beads of 50 pieces (a rosary) with gilded 'gaudies'.

St John of Bridlington was venerated throughout the country. There were altars dedicated to him at Dover and Sandwich and there are representations of the saint in 15th-century stained glass at Warwick, Ludlow, and Morley in Derbyshire and on a 15th-century screen at Hempstead, Norfolk.

The popularity of St John brought prosperity to the priory and the town as pilgrims flocked to the shrine. The high points were the royal visits in the early 15th century; firstly Henry IV in 1407 then Henry V, in 1421, with his new queen Catherine of Valois and his brother Humphrey, Duke of Gloucester. It is not known if Henry VI visited the shrine during his stay at Beverley in 1448, but he did own a finger of St John of Bridlington, which he gave to Eton College, and he granted the priory three fairs and exemptions from paying numerous taxes. It was not only royalty who favoured the priory for in 1409 the Pope granted the prior the jealously reserved right to wear a mitre and a pontifical ring.

'W Wodbus' inscribed on a cell wall in the Tower of London, possibly by Prior William Wood of Bridlington. *(From a rubbing by J.S. Purvis)*

The Pilgrimage of Grace

On 8 October 1536 John Smoothing, a governor of Beverley, arrived at Bridlington with news of an uprising that was to seal the fate of Bridlington Priory. Termed by its participants 'the Pilgrimage of Grace', this popular and, initially, highly successful rising against the government of Henry VIII had no single cause although it was partly a response to the suppression of the lesser monasteries. In the ten days after the first gathering at Beverley the people of the East Riding rose up in their thousands in response to the ringing of bells and firing of beacons.

The prior of Bridlington, William Wood, sent eleven horsemen and two of the canons, William Bromeflete and John Lamberte, to join the rebels and contributed over £10 to the cause. He also approved the actions of Dr John Pickering, a Dominican friar then staying at the priory, who wrote a rhyme encouraging the rebels. The steward of the priory, Sir Robert Constable of Flamborough, a 'troublous and dangerous' man with a grudge against the government, was recruited as one of the leaders of the rising.

Under the leadership of Robert Aske of Aughton, the rebels easily took York, Hull and Pontefract and a force of 30,000 advanced to Doncaster where they were confronted on 26 October by a royal army of 11,000 under the Duke of Norfolk. A truce was called and after lengthy discussions the rebels' requests for a general pardon and a parliament in the north to consider their grievances were agreed to. However in January 1537 Sir Francis Bigod of Settrington unwisely led a second short-lived rising which gave the king an excuse to take revenge on Aske and the other leaders of the Pilgrimage of Grace.

Amongst those arrested and charged with treason were Prior Wood of Bridlington and Sir Robert Constable. After imprisonment in the Tower of London, the prior was tried, found guilty and on 2 June 1537 was executed on the gallows on Knavesmire at York. In July Sir Robert Constable was hanged in chains outside Beverley Gate at Hull.

Bridlington Priory and all its possessions were forfeited to the Crown by the treason of Prior Wood and in May 1537 the process of its dissolution and destruction began.

Dissolution and destruction

The dissolution of the priory took place at the hands of Thomas Howard, Duke of Norfolk, who arrived at Bridlington, 'sore handled with his disease' on the evening of 16 May 1537. Two days later he wrote to Thomas Cromwell informing him that the goods of the priory had been 'viewed' and the best items had been sent to Sheriff Hutton. Although the duke made a plea for the retention of the shrine of St John of Bridlington as 'the people will be desirous to have it' he was instructed by Cromwell to demolish it. Soon afterwards all the gold work on the shrine was taken off, put into two boxes and sent to the king.

Bridlington Priory was reported as dissolved on 23 May and the next day Norfolk and his retinue set out for Jervaulx Abbey. With the canons and their servants dismissed, the great priory stood empty and unguarded. When Richard Pollard, the king's commissioner, arrived on 12 June he reported that Norfolk had taken 'all the jewels of the church, the vestments, the plate, oxen, and a great part of the sheep'. Pollard found more silver and gold in the church and sent it to the duke, and he sold the remaining sheep, cattle and household 'stuffe'. The last was the worst he had ever seen in 'any house of reputation' for 'a great part thereof was stolen by the poor people before my coming thither'. The priory buildings were surveyed by Pollard who found the 'house and church … far in decay' and that the chief profit would be made from the lead.

It was not until March 1538 that the priory buildings, with the exception of the nave of the church and the Bayle, were stripped of lead and largely demolished, and a new chapter in the history of Bridlington began.

48 High Street, Bridlington. *(Olga Reckitt)* The lower part of the façade is of reused stone from the demolished priory. There are numerous examples of reused priory stone in the Old Town.

Bridlington Priory church from the south east. Drawing by Fanny Waring 1805. *(F.F. Johnson)* The scars of the destruction can be clearly seen at the east and south sides of the church.

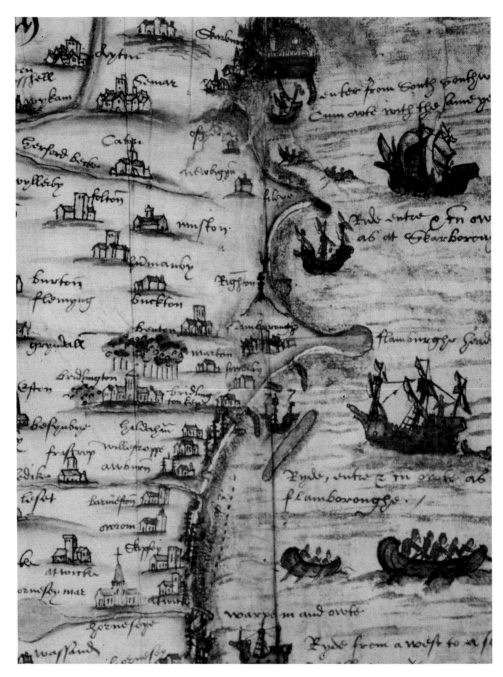

Detail from Lord Burghley's chart of the River Humber c. 1560 showing the East Yorkshire coast between Hornsea and Scarborough. *(By permission of The British Library – MS Royal 18/D III F62V.63)* The settlements of Bridlington and Bridlington 'Key' [Quay] are shown. The former has the Priory church represented with its central tower. The north and south piers are shown and the Smethwick Sands. Note also the piers and harbour at Flamborough and a beacon to the north. South of the Quay is a line of beacons from Hilderthorpe to Hornsea.

The Tudor town and port

Initially the dissolution of the priory must have been a severe blow to the people of Bridlington for as was noted in 1537 'the great part of the inhabitants' had 'their living' within the monastery. It was not a prosperous community. Pollard had reported in the same year that he had never seen 'so needy people in my life as are in these parts'. A large number of cottages were in decay and the harbour piers were in a dangerous state 'and like to be lost'.

Henry VIII, as lord of the manor, had the cottages and harbour repaired and there are signs that once freed from the tight control of the priory the town began to prosper. Entrepreneurs appeared, such as Richard Shippabotham who acquired the houses and land of the former Guild of the Blessed Virgin Mary and other property in the area. By the time of his death in 1565 he was the leading townsman despite being a recusant and clinging to the old faith. His son Robert was killed at Bridlington in 1579 in a fight with George Errington from Northumberland, perhaps a mariner or merchant.

Although farming remained the main occupation the numbers in processing trades increased. There were skinners, glovers, maltsters and brewers. Almost everyone seems to have had a malt kiln; there were 52 kilns in the Old Town by 1609. Malt and corn were the principal exports in the expanding coastal and overseas trade at the Quay. Towards the end of the 16th century cloth from the West Riding became a significant export to the Low Countries involving a number of woollen drapers, including William Hustler. Also using the port were a few fishermen. In 1558 John Awbrough, fisherman, bequeathed to his son 'my great cobble called the Gregorie of Bridlington Key'.

The harbour piers, battered by the seas, were in constant need of repair and the trade of the port fluctuated greatly but was probably on the increase until the 1590s. The same can be said of the population of the town. In 1537 there were said to be one and a half thousand 'howseling people' in the parish but whether this referred to the whole ecclesiastical parish, which seems most likely, or just the township of Bridlington is unclear. The muster roll of 1539 records 118 men of an age to bear arms at the Old Town and 22 at the Quay,

A cottage at Old Bridlington drawn by Henry Cave, July 1809. *(Bayle Museum Trust)* The houses of Tudor Bridlington were chiefly timber-framed and thatched. Some of those repaired in the late 1530s were cruck-framed. The house of the merchant Robert Copeland, who died in 1566, comprised a hall, parlour, chamber, kitchen and buttery. A carpenter, Richard Hodome, who died 1569, lived in a two-roomed house with hall and parlour and a workshop attached. The kitchen was often a separate building.

The Hustler arms on a ceiling at Acklam Hall, Middlesbrough. William Hustler made a fortune trading in West Riding cloth which he exported through Bridlington. As well as being active in the purchase of the manor he endowed the grammar school in 1636. He bought the Manor of Acklam (Middlesbrough) from Sir Matthew Boynton of Barmston in 1637.

The Corbett arms. William Corbett, the first Chief Lord of the Lords Feoffees of the Manor of Bridlington, was the son of Henry Corbett, steward of Sir Henry Griffith of Burton Agnes. Corbett accompanied Sir Henry from Staffordshire when he moved to Burton Agnes in the 1590s.

considerably more than the 49 men at Kilham. The parish registers which survive from 1564 indicate a marked rise in population until the late 1580s followed by a decline until the 1630s. This drop is partly due to a high death rate, with an outbreak of plague in 1588 and possibly again in 1605, but chiefly to economic decline.

The Manor of Bridlington

From the dissolution the Manor of Bridlington was in Crown hands and with it the responsibility for the upkeep of the harbour which became an increasing burden. In a report to Queen Elizabeth in 1562 the Marquis of Winchester, the High Treasurer, stated that despite continual expenditure on harbour repairs since 1537 the piers were in as much need of repair as ever. He recommended that the lands of the manor be let in return for a rent and an undertaking to repair the harbour.

In 1566 twelve inhabitants of Bridlington, headed by Thomas Waferer, who had married Richard Shippabotham's widow, took out a 40-year lease of the manor. They agreed to pay a rental of £152 17s. 5¾d. per year and to repair the piers within three years. For these repairs the lessees were granted £100, 120 oaks or other trees and 'all old stone at the site of the Monastery not yet sold'. Once again the ongoing costs of harbour repairs proved prohibitive and in 1585 the lease became void through failure to pay the rent.

In 1595 another group of thirteen leading townsmen, including the woollen draper William Hustler, concerned at the state of the piers, took on a 41-year lease on similar terms. They agreed to restore the harbour within two years and to choose twelve other tenants to be associated with them. In 1623, when the lease still had thirteen years to run, the manor was granted by King James I to Sir John Ramsey, Earl of Holderness. In 1600 Ramsey, then a young page to King James, killed the Master of Ruthven and the Earl of Gowrie when, it is claimed, they had threatened the life of the king. For this act Ramsey received numerous rewards including the Manor of Bridlington. On his death in 1625 the manor passed to his brother, Sir George Ramsey, who lived at Coldstream in the Scottish Borders.

When the townsmen at Bridlington heard five

years later that Ramsey was keen to sell the manor negotiations for its purchase were begun by two woollen drapers, William Corbett and John Hodgson, and two merchants Benjamin Jackson and Robert Prudom, with the assistance of William Hustler, the surviving original lessee of 1595. Two journeys were made to Newcastle-on-Tyne to consult with Sir George Ramsey and visits were made to London by the negotiators, the most active of whom was Benjamin Jackson. Tenants of the manor subscribed £4,200 for its purchase and on 30 June 1630 it was conveyed from Ramsey to thirteen feoffees or trustees.

The Lords Feoffees and the Great Town Deed

The principal reason why the townspeople clubbed together to buy the manor in 1630 was the desire of many to purchase the property they were renting. The joint purchase of the manor avoided 'the charge of a multiplicitie of conveyances' but this was only the first stage of the process. In 1636, after Benjamin Jackson had made at least four further journeys to London to consult documents, including the Domesday Book, and seemingly when the 1595 lease had come to an end, the so-called Great Town Deed was drawn up.

The deed, signed on 6 May 1636, was an agreement between the thirteen purchasers of the manor, the feoffees, and 187 tenants or freeholders of the manor. By the agreement the thirteen feoffees, namely William Corbett, Benjamin Jackson, John Hodgson, Robert Prudom, William Johnson, John Rickaby, Francis Palmer, Richard Staveley, John Gibbon, Thomas Jackson, Richard Milner, Robert Parkin and Robert Lyvock, were confirmed in their appointment as custodians of the manor and its property and they were to seek twelve assistants who were to be elected by the freeholders. When the number of Lords Feoffees, as they came to be known, was reduced to six their number was to be made up to thirteen from the ablest of the surviving assistants. Then an election was to be held for assistants. On 2 February each year one of the Lords Feoffees was to be chosen the Chief Lord who would then take out a lease of the manor for the year.

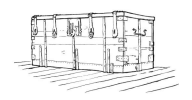

The 17th-century Town Chest (drawing by F.F.Johnson). The chest, preserved in the Court Room of the Bayle, contains the Great Town Deed, the original leases and many other documents.

A selection of 17th-century leases from the Town Chest. (Lords Feoffees) Some have decorated initial letters. By the terms of the Great Town Deed each signatory was to have their respective property 'conveyed and assured unto [them] ... for ever'. This was carried out by means of what are termed leases, of which there are some 200 for the years 1636-58.

A BRIEFE
RELATION
O F
The Remarkeable 'occur-
rences in the Northerne parts.;
Viz.
The Landing of the
QVEENES
MAIESTIE
In the Bay of BURLINGTON:
And
The repulse given unto the Rebels *at
the Towne of* NEWARK:
Both signified by severall Letters on the same day,
being *Friday March.* 3. 1642.

Printed by H.Hall. *M.DC.XLII.*

The cover of a Royalist pamphlet
published Friday 3 March 1642/3
reporting on Henrietta Maria's
landing at Bridlington. *(East
Riding of Yorkshire Council)*

Queen Henrietta Maria at Bridlington

Hardly had the townspeople of Bridlington become familiar with their newly acquired status when their lives were disrupted by the Civil Wars between King Charles I and Parliament. Isolated as they were from the main centres of the conflict they might have escaped involvement altogether except for a chance event in February 1643.

On 23 February 1642, before the outbreak of the first Civil War, Queen Henrietta Maria went to Holland with some of the Crown Jewels to raise money to buy arms and hire troops for the Royalist cause. While she was there Parliament sent Walter Strickland, brother of Sir William Strickland of Boynton, as ambassador to Holland to thwart her activities. He was unsuccessful and on 19 January 1643 Queen Henrietta Maria set sail for England accompanied by eleven ships filled with troops, ammunition and stores. The convoy was caught in a tremendous gale and after nine days, and the loss of two ships, was forced to return to the Dutch coast.

A fortnight later they set out again with Newcastle as the intended destination. However, on Monday 20 February, as they neared the English coast at Scarborough, the wind began to blow from the north and 'they fell back into a Safe-Harbour (Burlington-Bay) and cast anchor hard by the shore'. A message was sent at once to the Earl of Newcastle, the commander-in-chief of the Royalist forces in northern England, who happened to be with his army at Pocklington, 26 miles from Bridlington, on his way to attack Hull. He despatched a force and on the afternoon of Wednesday 22 February 1000 Royalist horsemen appeared on the beach at Bridlington. That night Henrietta Maria and her entourage, including the Duchess of Richmond and the dwarf Sir Jeffrey Hudson, landed and she was lodged in a house above the harbour. The following day the Earl of Newcastle arrived with a further 1500 horsemen and over 1000 foot soldiers.

Between five and six o'clock the next morning, 24 February, four Parliamentary ships sailed in close to the harbour and fired their guns for two hours at the Quay. The Queen was forced to leave her lodgings and as Sir Henry Slingsby recorded: 'The Queen and the Duchess of Richmond and the rest of the Ladies, to save themselves from shott, gott under the bank of a little gullet of water [the Gypsey Race] that runs into the sea...here having cloakes cast under them, and about them did the Ladies sit and take notice without danger where every bullet grazed.'

Nearby lay the body of a soldier 'torn and mangled with their great shott'. As the Queen fled from her lodgings she remembered that she had left her lap-dog, Mitte, behind. She quickly returned and gathered the dog from her bed before gaining the safety of the ditch.

Eventually the Dutch admiral, Tromp, who had escorted the Queen from Holland, drove the Parliamentary ships away. At noon Henrietta Maria removed to the Old Town where she may have been accommodated at William Hustler's house in High Street, the largest in the town. The arms and ammunition, said to be for 12,000 men, were unloaded from the ships and carried to the Priory church where they were carefully stored. The following Sunday the parishioners were understandably encouraged to go to services in neighbouring villages or to attend 'the Queenes Court, where by Her Majesties leave her household had service and sermon ... At this, the Country People wondered much, who believed all with the Queen to be Papists'.

Henrietta Maria was at Bridlington for nearly two weeks, during which time she was visited by the Earl of Montrose and other Scottish sympathisers and also by the Parliamentarian John Hotham from Hull. Hotham's intrigues with the Royalists led to his execution, and the execution of his father.

On the afternoon of Sunday 5 March, after much delay whilst transport for the arms and ammunition was arranged, the Queen finally set out for York.

The Queen's House, Queen Street, Bridlington. *(F. F. Johnson)* This house, demolished 1894, was by tradition the house where Henrietta Maria lodged. Its site is now occupied by the Harbour Lites. In 1643 it was probably the most westerly house at the Quay. The lower part could be early 17th century but it appears to have been heightened and much altered in the 18th century.

Queen Henrietta Maria. A
portrait formerly at Boynton
Hall. By tradition this portrait
was left by the Queen in return
for the Strickland family plate
which she had taken after staying
at the Hall. The houses and lands
of Sir William Strickland, a
leading Parliamentarian, were
plundered by the Royalist troops
from Bridlington but there is no
evidence for the Queen's visit
to Boynton. She did stay at Sir
Henry Griffith's fine 'new' house
at Burton Agnes during her time
at Bridlington. Queen Henrietta
Maria retained an affection for
Bridlington and when, in 1665,
she helped Richard Boyle, 2nd
Earl of Cork obtain an earldom
in the English peerage, it was to
please the Queen Dowager that
he chose the title of Burlington.

A vast convoy of 500 waggons left Bridlington accompanied by the army. The first night was spent at
Burton Fleming and the next at Malton. Late on the
afternoon of Tuesday 7 March the Queen entered
York where she remained until 3 June when she left
for Oxford.

Henrietta Maria's landing at Bridlington
brought the town national prominence and had
repercussions, both short and long term. It was
later claimed that the town had been 'very much
impoverished by the unhappy landing of the
Queen' and 'by the cruelty of Lord Newcastle's
Army' in burning the timber set aside for repair-
ing the harbour.

The Battle of Bridlington

A Royalist garrison was left at Bridlington and
this became the target of Parliamentary troops
from Hull in early 1644. A contemporary newslet-
ter describes the actions of their commander, Sir
William Constable, who was no stranger to
the area he having once owned the manor of
Flamborough:

'Constable with ten troops of horse and two
hundred foot souldiers, hath taken Birdlington [sic]
… at his approach thereunto the enemies musket-
eers that were Garrisoned there issued out to en-
counter him; but he made his foot wheele about
and get between the Towne and them and then
charged them with his horse in the front, and his
foot also charged them in the Reare he easily rout-
ed them and took one hundred and fifty nine under
officers and common souldiers, as also one Sarjant
Major, one Captain who was an Irish man and one
Lieutenant and he took also as some report six
small ships in the bay, that were laden with Wooll
and other commodities and going to Holland.'

The date of the 'Battle of Bridlington' is uncer-
tain but was probably around 6-7 February 1644.
Bridlington was afterwards garrisoned by Parliament and it became a base for attacks on Scarborough. During the Civil Wars Bridlington was
taxed heavily and troops, first Royalist then Parliamentarian, were billeted at the Old Town and
the Quay. A whole series of billeting papers survives in the town chest in the Bayle including a list
of 46 householders and the 51 soldiers billeted on
them. The leading merchant William Bower ac-

commodated four soldiers in his house, two of them for four weeks, and Thomas Rickaby had two for two weeks.

The fort

The landing of Queen Henrietta Maria highlighted Bridlington Bay's strategic importance and the necessity of providing defences at the Quay. In late February 1643, after the attack by the Parliamentary ships, the Royalists fortified the harbour with small cannons mounted on batteries on either side of the harbour.

During the Commonwealth and Restoration periods the actions of Dunkirkers (privateers) and the Dutch continued the need for fortifications. In July 1667, during the second Dutch war, a fort armed with fifteen guns was built on the north side of the harbour, and a garrison established with Sir Robert Hildyard as governor. Peace was concluded almost immediately and in September the guns and ammunition from 'that complete and well-finished fort' were ordered to be sent to London. The fort was reported as being in decay at the outbreak of the third Dutch war in 1672, but six years later it was repaired and a force of 100 men, with a lieutenant, an ensign, three serjeants, three corporals and two drummers was installed with Sir John Reresby as governor. Although Reresby retained his governorship until 1689 there was 'neither company nor gunner at Bridlington' by November 1680 and the guns were removed in 1688.

A sketch of the North Fort at Bridlington by J.S. Purvis from a painting now at Sewerby Hall. Part of Fort Hall is shown on the left. *(East Riding of Yorkshire Council)*

The drawbridge and guardhouse at the Fort, Bridlington drawn by Henry Cave, July 1809. *(East Riding of Yorkshire Council)*

Anno Octavo & Nono

Gulielmi III. Regis.

An Act for the Repair of the Peers of Bridlington alias *Burlington*, in the East-Riding of the County of York.

Wheras the Bay of Bridlington *alias* Burlington, in the East-Riding in the County of York, is a Spacious, Safe and Secure Bay for His Majesties and all other Ships or Uessels, Trading or Sailing upon that Coast, or to or from the Northward, and the Port or Peer of Bridlington *alias* Burlington, (While it was in Repair) was of great Use and Advantage to His Majesties and other Ships Passing to or from the Northwards, or Trading upon that Coast, for their necessary Supply of Fresh Water, Uictuals Ommmmmm and

The title page of the 1697 act which established the Harbour Commissioners.

Bridlington Key from the south by Francis Place of York, c. 1720. (© *British Museum*) This, the earliest view of the port, shows that some of the houses had shaped or Dutch gables.

A new fort was ordered to be built in 1748 but by the 1760s the 'fort houses' were being used to accommodate the poor of the town. Following attacks by privateers in the bay the fort was armed with seven twelve-pounder canons in 1779. Finally in 1794, during the French Revolutionary war, a moat was dug around the fort on the north side, and a battery was constructed to the southwest of the Quay in Hilderthorpe. The south fort fell into the sea c. 1805 and much of the north fort suffered the same fate in 1813.

The harbour

Despite the trials of the Anglo-Dutch wars and the depredations of privateers, the town and port of Bridlington benefited greatly by the trade boom of the 1660s-80s. The chief concern remained, as always, the state of the piers.

In December 1663 the greater part of the harbour 'being built of timber was broken down and ruined … by a violent and tempestuous rage of the sea'. Again in November 1696 much of the North Pier was thrown down in a storm and the remainder was 'in imminent danger of being utterly ruined, and the whole port or peer utterly lost, and thereby the said port and bay become of little or no use'.

The necessary action was taken promptly. Early in 1697 an act of parliament was passed which ordered the levying of 'one farthing for every chaldron of coals [the Newcastle chaldron was about 50 cwt.] that shall be loaden on board any ship, hoy, bark or other vessel, at or in the port of Newcastle upon Tyne' and its member ports, including Sunderland and Blyth. The preamble to the act stated that the port of Bridlington was of 'great use and advantage to His Majesties and other ships passing to or from the northwards, or trading upon the coast, for their necessary supply of freshwater, victuals and provisions of all sorts, security of ships in time of war, as also from storms'. The act was periodically renewed and, from the income received by the Harbour Commissioners appointed under the act, the piers were regularly repaired and twice rebuilt.

The trade of the port

In a broadsheet entitled *The Case of Bridlington-Peer,* c. 1664, the port was said to be used for the 'exporting of grain, and other inland commodities, and for the importation of coals, salt, firrwood and other timber' as well as supplying fresh water, and 'necessary provisions and victuals' to naval and merchant vessels. It was also 'very

The late 17th-century die for the seal of the collector of customs at Bridlington. (*Lords Feoffees*) The inscription is SI:BRIDLINGTON. MEM: DE'P:KINGS:SUPER. HULL meaning 'the seal of Bridlington a member of the port of Kingston upon Hull'. The seal bears a thistle above a barrel, a pun on the name Burlington, the thistle being a 'burr' in Scots and the barrel a 'tun' thus 'bur-on-tun'.

Bridlington harbour looking west from the North Pier. A late 18th-century view by Francis Nicholson (1753-1844). *(East Riding of Yorkshire Council)* The wooden South Pier, on the left, had been rebuilt on new foundations 1719-55.

Trade token of Nicholas Woolfe, haberdasher, 1665. There were four generations of Woolfes, merchants, mariners, woollen drapers and haberdashers in Bridlington.

commodious for the fishing trade, and especially in the time of the herring-fishing every year; during which time, boats and other vessels resort thither, from Whitby, Robin-hood's Bay, Scarborough, and several other places; whereby the city of York, Hull, Beverley, and all the country adjacent, is plentifully supplyed'.

This neatly summarises the trade of the port in the late 17th century. Much more detail is provided by the port books in the Public Record Office which record the imports and exports of the coastal and foreign trade as well as the names of the ships, their masters and the merchants trading in them. The greater part of the trade was coastal, mainly carrying coal and salt from Sunderland and Newcastle. In 1667 there were 49 outward sailings and 39 inward. In 1685 this figure had risen to 103 outward and 134 inward dropping back to 40 outward and 81 inward in 1722. Overseas sailings, carrying cloth, corn and malt to the Low Countries and the Baltic, and importing timber, were less numerous. There were 37 outward sailings and 24 inward in 1687 and 24 outward and fifteen inward in 1721-22. The 1670s-80s was a boom period for the port of Bridlington, and its trade exceeded that of Scarborough.

Merchants and shipping

The trade of Bridlington in the years 1660-1730 was dominated by the merchant families of Bower, Hudson, Prudom, Rickaby, Wilson and Woolfe and the occasional successful individual such as the Quaker Richard Hardcastle. The first four families listed were well established and were in the town in the 16th century. The Woolfes had also been in Bridlington at that time, but Nicholas Woolfe, haberdasher, founder of the merchant dynasty, came from Scarborough c. 1625. Hardcastle came from the West Riding and Thomas Wilson from Thirsk c. 1675. The merchant families were linked by trade and marriage to each other and to the merchant communities of Hull, Leeds, Whitby, Scarborough and York as well as the north-east ports.

To spread the risk the merchants held shares in ships rather than owning whole ships. When John Rickaby made his will in 1700 he had shares in 21 Bridlington ships; in two he had a 1/8th share, in eight a 1/16th share and in eleven a 1/32nd share.

The merchants' activities were carefully scrutinised by the customs officials from their customs house at the Quay. In 1700 Richard Woolfe was imprisoned in York Castle for three years for illegally shipping malt to Rotterdam. Letters sent to London from Thomas Aslaby, collector of customs, in the 1670s provide much information on the affairs of the port including the visit of the English fleet in 1672 commanded by the future King James II. Much money was made at this time in supplying the fleet, and between four and five hundred men were landed 'most of them afflicted with scurvy'.

The merchant community

The trade boom of the later 17th and early 18th century was the making of Bridlington. Its legacy is the wealth of fine houses, some disguised by later changes, which line High Street and Westgate. These include The Toft, 43 High Street, built in 1673 by William Hudson, merchant, who was then Chief Lord, and 7-9 Westgate rebuilt in 1682 by Hudson's son-in-law, Thomas Wilson, merchant. The new houses of the 1670s-80s springing up in the Old Town and the Quay were of brick and pantile, the latter coming into the port from Holland.

Late 17th-century staircase at The Toft, 43 High Street, Bridlington.

Centre bay of 7-9 Westgate, Bridlington (Hebblethwaite House). Rebuilt 1682. An artisan-mannerist house with fine brickwork detail and original casement windows. *(Georgian Society for East Yorkshire)*

There was another boom in building at the end of Queen Anne's reign. At this date the merchant Giles Rickaby built his mansion at the Quay, on Prince Street. (see p.118) In 1735 Thomas Gent described the Quay as 'very beautiful town, having houses fronting each other like a street'. The Rickaby mansion has gone and little remains of the early 18th-century Quay. Three contemporary houses survive elsewhere: Bestworth House, High Street built c. 1712 by Allan Lamont, customs collector, the Avenue, Westgate built 1714 by John Grimston and Sewerby Hall (originally Sewerby House) built at much the same date by John Greame who had moved from the High Street. Grimston was a highly successful attorney. He kept a coach and owned much land in the neighbourhood. His bitter enemy was Greame, a former client with origins in farming and trade, who had married wisely (twice).

The merchants, attorneys, apothecaries and leading tradesmen provided Bridlington with a social and cultural community that in a minor way mirrored that of a county town. In the early 18th century the town could boast a bookseller, a library at the church, a bowling green, a cockpit, a potential spa, and possibly a town hunt.

The merchants travelled to York and London, for pleasure as well as business. They subscribed to books, to the assembly rooms at York, and to good causes such as the new flooring at York Minster designed by William Kent (see below), and often made charitable bequests. Their sons might go to Cambridge University or be apprenticed to successful relatives in London. Many went to the grammar school in the Bayle then flourishing with University-trained masters including the indigent author Richard Fiddes, associate of Jonathan Swift.

As elsewhere Bridlington's most successful merchants and professionals bought country estates and joined the landed society. Leonard Bower, who spent some time in Stockholm as a young man, bought an estate at Scorton, North Yorkshire and his descendants lived at Welham

The grave slab of William Bower, merchant, died March 1671/2, in the Priory church. He founded the Knitting School.

Sir John Major, Bt. M.P. of Worlingworth, Suffolk by Sir Joshua Reynolds. *(Lord Henniker)* Born at Bridlington Quay, John Major, master mariner, moved to Wapping on the River Thames around 1720. There he became an elder of Trinity House and the leading merchant in the iron trade with Sweden. He made a fortune and bought estates in Sussex and Suffolk, was granted a baronetcy and represented Scarborough in Parliament. He married Ann, the daughter of Daniel Dale of Bridlington, and they had two daughters, one of whom became the first Lady Henniker and the other the Duchess of Chandos. The family retained property in the town until the 19th century.

The grave of Robert Prudom, merchant (died 1708), in the Baptist burial ground, Applegarth Lane. It is doubtful if the small building in the burial ground was originally a Baptist chapel. The first Baptist meeting house licensed in 1709 was next to the Bayle, where there is another burial ground.

The Friends Meeting House, St John Street, by William Fallowes. *(Lords Feoffees)* Built by 1700 the meeting house ceased to be registered as a place of worship in 1861. The Quakers had a burial ground in Havelock Street.

Hall, near Malton. The Hudsons bought the Bessingby estate, built the hall and married into the aristocracy and the Grimstons moved to Neswick Hall. Only the Rickabys clung tenaciously to their roots and remained in their house at the Quay until the 1860s.

Nonconformity

John Major and his family were members of the Independent Chapels at Bridlington and Wapping and as dissenters from the Anglican church they were typical of the urban trading community. In 1665 sixteen of the leading townsmen, including merchants, master mariners, woollen drapers, a maltster and a skinner, went to Flamborough church, where the incumbent of the Priory church was taking a service, and they sat throughout with their hats on!

In 1675 Aslaby, the customs collector, reported that 'the Quakers and other Dissenters meet frequently in great numbers'. The Quakers (Society of Friends) were meeting in the town by 1652. In 1660 five Bridlington Quakers were imprisoned in York Castle. Amongst them was Robert Fowler, a master mariner, who in 1657-8 had taken a group of Quakers to America in his small ship the *Woodhouse*.

The Independents (later Presbyterians then Congregationalists) had their origins in a group

that formed around the Revd William Lucke, an Anglican clergyman ejected from his living at Bridlington in 1662. Lucke was given permission in 1672 to hold services in the Bayle. One of his followers Robert Prudom, a former Quaker, founded the Baptist church in Bridlington in 1698.

Old Dissent was in decline when Methodism was introduced into Bridlington in 1769. John Wesley visited the town the following year and on nine further occasions, the last in 1790. Methodist meeting houses were licensed on St John Street and King Street by 1775. Primitive Methodism arrived in 1821 and chapels were built on St John Street and the Esplanade in 1833.

William Kent

Bridlington's most famous son, William Kent, the great 18th-century architect and designer of interiors, furniture and landscapes, was born in 1685. His father William Cant, joiner, built or rebuilt 45 High Street, Bridlington in 1693. Here the future architect must have spent part of his childhood. Showing talent as a painter he went to London where in February 1709, as William Cant, 'limner' [a painter], he witnessed three deeds by which Susanna Prudom, widow of a Bridlington merchant, and her eldest son Robert Prudom of London, mercer, conveyed land in Bridlington.

Three months later, using his newly adopted surname 'Kent', he was taken to see the Secretary of State by Sir William Hustler of Acklam, North Riding. Hustler, who had property in the High Street, Bridlington was the grandson of William Hustler, the wealthy draper who endowed the grammar school, brother-in-law of Sir Richard Osbaldeston of Hunmanby, and uncle of Sir William Wentworth of Bretton, Kent's first known patron. It was almost certainly these three, Hustler, Osbaldeston and Wentworth, who helped Kent get to Italy in 1709.

Kent spent ten years in Italy, returning with Richard, third Earl of Burlington, whom he had met in Rome. Burlington, the great patron of the arts and a skilled architect, first promoted Kent as a 'history-painter' and interior designer securing him commissions from the king and other members of the Court. From 1730 Kent, who had become a member of Burlington's household, turned

Datestone at the rear of 45 High Street, Bridlington. *(D. Neave)* The initials stand for William and Esther Cant, William Kent's parents. On William Cant's death in 1739 the house passed to Kent's sister Esther, then to her daughter Mary, successively the wife of Thomas Stead and Thomas Dale.

William Kent by Benedetto Luti *(by permission of the Trustees of the Chatsworth Settlement).* Painted in Rome in 1718 when Kent was 32. He died at Burlington House, Piccadilly on 12 April 1748 and in his will he makes bequests to his sister in Bridlington and her three children.

his attention to architecture and here he excelled. He was also a highly accomplished furniture designer, but his greatest contribution was as one of the founders of English landscape gardening.

Shipbuilding

In the mid-17th century many Bridlington merchants had ships built at Hull or Newcastle, but some shipbuilding was taking place at the Quay. The Quaker Robert Fowler is said to have built his ship the *Woodhouse* at Bridlington before 1657, and William Blakelock is described as a 'shipwright' in a deed dated 1662. A shipbuilding dock is mentioned at the Quay in 1682 and the names of sixteen shipwrights or ship carpenters are recorded in Bridlington parish registers in the years 1710-40. These include Robert Milner who in 1700 was building a 'pink' (a small sea-going vessel) for the merchant John Rickaby.

Shipbuilding took place at the entrance to Clough Hole. It was at a shipyard here that 40 or more ships were built between 1770 and 1843 by a succession of shipwrights including James and Francis Ellis, Joseph, Thomas and William Nelson Heward, John Simpson, George Gray and James Day. The greatest activity was during the years 1791-1801 and 1811-15, the period of the French Revolutionary and Napoleonic Wars. The majority of ships built at Bridlington were square-sterned brigantines, but barques, sloops, snows and schooners were also built. The largest recorded ship built at the port was the 325-ton *Albion*, built in 1793 for the whaling trade. The last Bridlington-built ship was the schooner *Queen Dowager* built by James Day early in 1843.

The Battle of Flamborough Head

On the evening of Thursday 23 September 1779 there occurred within sight of Bridlington one of the most famous naval engagements to have taken place off the English coast, the Battle of Flamborough Head. It was fought between the *Bonhomme Richard*, a 34-gun frigate under the command of John Paul Jones, a Scotsman who had been commissioned by the American government to harass English shipping during the American War of Independence, and the 44-gun frigate *HMS Serapis* of the Royal Navy commanded by Captain Richard Pearson.

Shipbuilding on the north side of Langdale's Wharf in the 1830s. A watercolour by O.W. Kilvington. *(East Yorkshire Museums Service)*

The Active of Bridlington by William Ward of Hull, 1800. *(Bayle Museum Trust)* Probably *The Active,* a square-sterned brigantine, built at Bridlington by Francis Ellis in 1788. She was taken by the French in 1794.

The Battle of Flamborough Head. Painting by an unknown artist. *(Lords Feoffees)*

John Paul Jones by Jean Michel Moreau, 1780. Regarded as the 'Father of the American Navy' John Paul Jones died in Paris in 1792. In 1913 his body which had lain in an unmarked French grave was reburied in a magnificent marble sarcophagus at Annapolis Naval Academy.

On the afternoon of the battle Jones was in Bridlington Bay with his squadron of three frigates and a brig when a convoy of 41 English merchant ships was spotted travelling southwards towards Flamborough Head under the protection of Captain Pearson. Although night was falling Jones, in his usual fashion, advanced on the convoy and at about 7.20 p.m., just to the north of Flamborough Head, the first shots were fired between the vastly superior *HMS Serapis* and the *Bonhomme Richard*. A close and bitter battle ensued for more than three hours during which over 100 men were killed and both ships were severely damaged. The battle had been going in Pearson's favour when a violent explosion wrecked the gundeck of the *Serapis*. Pearson thereupon surrendered and Jones took over his ship abandoning the *Bonhomme Richard* which eventually sank at 10.30 a.m. on Saturday 25 September.

The sounds of the battle were clearly heard at Bridlington. The firing guns and flames from the burning ships dramatically lit up the night sky. An eyewitness reported that 'the cliffs were thronged with spectators and the Quay was in an indescribable state of pandemonium'.

The open fields

Although agriculture played a part in the lives of almost all the inhabitants of Bridlington in the 17th and 18th centuries there were few for whom farming was their sole source of income. Between 30 and 40 people owned land, but the farming units were small and the farming system was still much as it had been in the middle ages.

The plan opposite, based on information provided in the enclosure award of 1771, attempts to reconstruct the field system of Bridlington in the mid-18th century. At this time some 2,010 acres (814 ha.) of the parish, that is 80% of the land, was still held in common and regulated by the manor court. The arable land lay in four large open fields to the north of the town, West Field, Hill Field, Ducky Dike Field and East Field, each between 200 and 300 acres in extent. Under the open-field system individual owners would have their land, possibly in narrow strips, distributed throughout the arable fields. The system at Bridlington is unclear but by the 18th century there

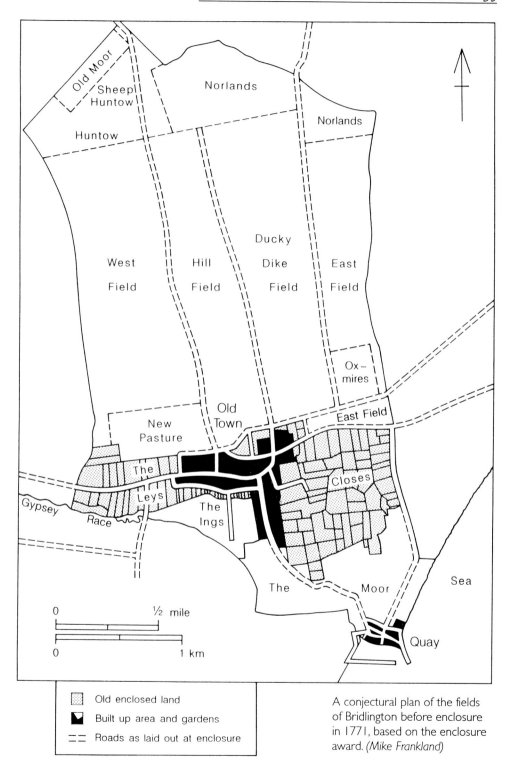

Old enclosed land

Built up area and gardens

Roads as laid out at enclosure

A conjectural plan of the fields of Bridlington before enclosure in 1771, based on the enclosure award. *(Mike Frankland)*

had been some re-organisation and land was held in units of three or five acre 'oxgangs'. Owners and tenants would also have rights of grazing livestock on the commons, on any open-field land left fallow, and on other open-field land after harvest.

The common grazing land of Bridlington lay in four blocks. Between the Old Town and the Quay was the Moor which covered some 160 acres. On the high wolds at the north end of the township were some 260 acres of common pasture called Huntow, Old Moor and Norlands. Here sheep and cattle were grazed and whins (gorse) gathered for fuel. Two other smaller areas of pasture, Oxmires (c. 20 acres) and New Pasture (c. 40 acres), carved out of the open fields, lay east and west of the Old Town. Between the town and the Gypsey Race were the Ings, some 50 acres of common meadowland.

There were two areas of closes or small hedged fields, some long enclosed. The large area of closes south-east of the Old Town would have been the demesne ('home farm') land of the priory. The closes known as the Leys to the west of the town, and at its western edge as Haverdale Heads were still subject to some common rights up to 1771. About 130 people had common rights at Bridlington; some 90 of these had no land but had the rights through ownership of a cottage. Every cottager had two beast-gates (right to graze) on the Moor and ten sheep-gates in Huntow and other commons.

The system worked well but in the late 1760s, with pressure for greater agricultural productivity and independence, an agreement was reached by the freeholders to enclose the open fields.

Enclosure of the open fields

In 1768 Parliament passed an act for enclosing the open fields, lands, meadows, pastures, commons and wastes of the township of Bridlington. Under the act three commissioners, Edward Cleaver from Ganthorpe, North Riding, John Outram from Burton Agnes and Peter Nevill of Benningholme Grange and two surveyors, Charles Tate of Hull and Joseph Dickinson of Beverley were appointed to carry out the enclosure. The township was surveyed and over

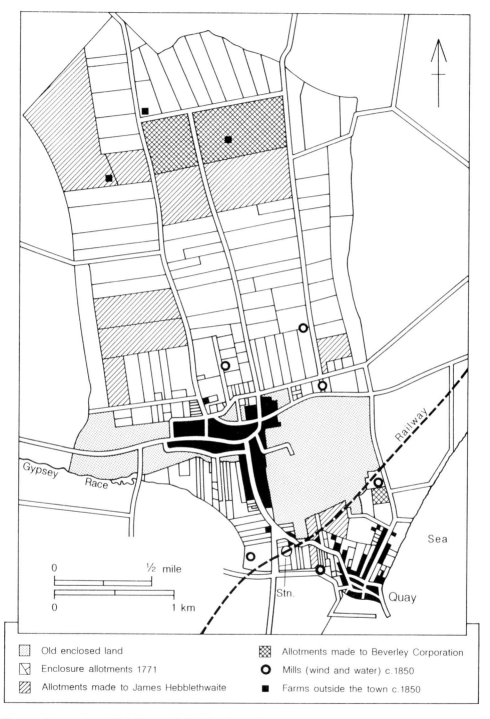

Old enclosed land		Allotments made to Beverley Corporation	
Enclosure allotments 1771		Mills (wind and water) c.1850	
Allotments made to James Hebblethwaite		Farms outside the town c.1850	

Post-enclosure plan of Bridlington. *(Mike Frankland)* Based on the enclosure plan with information from the first edition Ordnance Survey plan 6" to the mile, surveyed 1850, published 1854.

Limekiln, Bridlington by William Fallowes. *(Lords Feoffees)* Lime was used for spreading on the land as well as for mortar.

Dukes Mill, Bempton Lane. Built 1823 by Moses Duke. Probably not used after First World War.*(East Riding of Yorkshire Council)*

the next three years the commissioners had numerous meetings to sort out the claims, objections and requests of the various landowners and commoners. On 1 July 1771 they signed their award. The award is accompanied by a plan showing the location of each allotment and, as the earliest surviving plan of Bridlington, it is invaluable.

The largest amount of land was awarded to James Hebblethwaite, who received a total of 422 acres in fifteen allotments ranging in size from four perches to 135 acres. Hebblethwaite, from Norton-on-Derwent, had come to live at Bridlington after he had purchased the rectory estate in 1759. This gave him the right to the great tithes which were valued at £385 per annum in 1771. As owner of the rectory he received 265 acres in lieu of half the tithes, and an allotment of 157 acres in his own right. The second largest award of 139 acres was made to Beverley Corporation as trustees for the Ann Routh charity. By her will proved 1722 Ann Routh had left land in Bridlington to endow an almshouse in Beverley. There were eight awards of between 50 and 100 acres, the largest being that to Francis Coverley of Hilderthorpe of 84 acres, 26 awards of ten to 49 acres, 20 awards of between three and ten acres, 43 of between one and three acres and 56 of less than an acre. The last two groups would be awards to landless cottagers receiving allotments in lieu of their common rights.

The enclosure commissioners also awarded the township land for a gravel pit on the Moor (Midway Green) and two plots on the wolds for digging stone to repair the roads. They laid out the roads of the township, the majority at a width of 60 feet (18 m.). Some were 'ancient' roads such as 'Key Road' between the Quay and the south end of St John Street but others were seemingly new like Bempton Lane with its broad verges.

Within a short time of the signing of the enclosure award the landscape of Bridlington was transformed. Wide straight roads divided up the township and rectangular hedged fields replaced the bleakness of the open fields and commons. Eventually farmsteads appeared on the wolds and mills and other buildings were dotted about the fields. The Quay, just emerging as a resort, was at last able to break out of its restricted area.

The rise of the resort

By the 1760s the port of Bridlington was in decline. Its overseas trade had almost ceased and the import of coal and export of corn and malt had declined. Inland Driffield was challenging Bridlington's position as the chief corn market of the area. Then fortuitously the Quay was saved by what has been termed 'the rush to the sea' — the fashion for sea bathing.

For some years the inhabitants of Bridlington must have looked enviously at the rising fortunes of their nearby rival Scarborough. Here the 'spaw' or spa had been attracting gentry and merchant families in increasing numbers since the 1660s and its success reached a high point in the 1730s. It may not be a coincidence that it was in the early 1730s that an 'incomparable new Spaw' was discovered near the seashore just south of Bridlington. In 1738 it was reported that Bridlington was 'making a push' and had advertised its spa water. The success of the medicinal spring was short lived and it was a further 30 years before visitors started flocking to the Quay by which time sea bathing was all the rage.

The start of it all can be dated to the summer of 1765 when an advertisement headed 'Bathing Houses at Bridlington' appeared in the *York Courant* newspaper which stated:

'Complaint having been made for some time of the want of conveniences at Bridlington for bathing, and of the roughness of the shore on the North Sands; this is to acquaint gentlemen and ladies who require sea-bathing that commodious houses drawn by horses, and all other accommodations as at Scarborough, are now completed and ready for their reception, and a convenient road made for carriages to go down to the South Sands, which are as firm and free from stones as any sands in England.'

The following year the landlord of the Ship Inn at the Quay advertised that he had 'lately erected an Assembly Room' ready for 'the ensuing bathing season'. A week later there was published in the *York Courant* an extract from a letter from 'Burlington-Key' reporting that on the evening of Wednesday 25 June 1766 'the new Assembly-Room' had been opened by a 'large and genteel company, amongst whom were Sir Griffith Boynton ... and other gentlemen of fortune and distinction'.

'Bridlington is a little sea-port, which is supported by a slight trade that maintains ten or a dozen ships, and by the resort of some company to the quay for bathing.'

Arthur Young, 1769

Sir Christopher and Lady Sykes by George Romney. *(Sir Tatton Sykes Bt)*

Flat Top Farm, Bridlington. Built by Christopher Sykes in 1776, demolished 1966. *(East Riding of Yorkshire Council)*

Fort Hall, Bridlington Quay.
(East Riding of Yorkshire Council)
Another lost Georgian seaside
villa, built c. 1792 for John
Walker of Fairburn, near
Pontefract. It stood overlooking
the sea at the end of Fort
Terrace. Demolished 1937.

Bathing Machines at Bridlington
from George Walker, *The
Costume of Yorkshire*, 1814. *(East
Riding of Yorkshire Council)* Walker
noted that the bathing machines
on the Yorkshire coast differed 'in
several respects from those in
the more southern districts, and
particularly in their having no
awning to screen the bathers
from the public eye. This
frequently occasions very
ludicrous scenes.'

In 1767 William Standish, a London innkeeper, purchased two houses at Bridlington Quay and was soon advertising lodgings for the bathing season. John Grimston of Kilnwick Hall, near Driffield, rented lodgings from Standish for two months in 1772 when he took his ailing daughter Fanny to bathe on the recommendation of her York doctor. His son Henry, home from Harrow because of illness, was at the Quay three years later and he wrote home that he had 'supped at Bridlington upon chops and pickles and tart and about half past 9 we went to bed, got up at half past 7, went into the sea, came home, breakfasted, then went and took Lodgings at Mrs Standishes, found there a Tellescope, looked throw it at some ships'.

The resort soon became the preferred destination for the gentry families of the East Riding. One early and frequent visitor was Christopher Sykes (later the 2nd baronet), with his young family, from Sledmere. They were there in 1774 and again in August 1775 when Sykes spent £41. Such expenditure, partly on lodgings, no doubt encouraged him to build his own seaside accommodation. On his estate at Hilderthorpe, just to the south of the Quay, he built a charming belvedere or summer retreat in 1776. The house, later known as Flat Top Farm, had a magnificent view of the bay from the octagonal saloon on the first floor.

'I liked Bridlington Key very much.' So wrote John Courtney, a wealthy gentleman from Beverley, after a month's stay in 1796. A frequent visitor in the years 1788-1804, Courtney stayed at one or other of the numerous lodging houses at the Quay. Familiar from his youth with all the pleasures and amenities of London, Bath, Scarborough and Harrogate he far preferred Bridlington in his middle age. His diaries record his family bathing, walking on the sands or pier, taking tea with 'several agreeable people', playing cards and dancing in the assembly rooms at the Ship Inn and going to the theatre.

Bridlington acquired all the trappings of a resort town. In 1801 'commodious sea water, warm, cold and shower Baths' had been built 'adjoining the sea'. Theatrical performances were provided each year for over twenty years from c. 1805 by the company of William Smedley, a theatrical manager from Lincolnshire. It was he who fitted up the theatre in the Rope Walk, to the north of Chapel Street. There was a subscription library and billiard rooms by 1813. Ten years later Baines' *Directory* lists two booksellers, four lapidaries, three circulating libraries, a dancing master and a miniature painter as well as recording a 'chalybeate spring issuing out of a pleasant garden near the subscription-mills [near the corner of Station Road and Bessingby Road] the medicinal properties of which resemble the chalybeate springs of Scarborough and Cheltenham'.

In July 1829 the *Hull Advertiser* reported that 'This delightful resort of rank and fashion is already enlivened by the presence of much company, and the great improvements which have been made in the place will doubtless cause an accession of numbers to the gay assemblage'. The improvements included the Esplanade which had 'a spacious Colonnade, in which visitors, for a trifling expense, are accommodated with newspapers, etc.'.

The leading resorts of the south, Brighton and Weymouth, owed their success to Royal patronage. This eluded Bridlington, although in 1785 the future King William IV did stay at the Ship Inn when as a serving midshipman his ship was at anchor in Bridlington Bay. What was remembered of his visit was that a chambermaid, Sally Gibson, slapped the Prince's face when he attempted to

Bridlington's Georgian Theatre, Rope Walk. *(Norman Creaser)* This unassuming building survived until the 1980s.

A

DESCRIPTION

OF

BURLINGTON-KEY,

AND THE

NEIGHBOURHOOD.

By JAMES COATES,

LABOURER, BURLINGTON-KEY.

PRINTED FOR THE AUTHOR
BY H. MOZLEY, MARKET-PLACE, GAINSBOROUGH.
1805.

[Price Threepence.]

The cover of the first guide book to Bridlington which was in verse. The publisher Henry Mozley for a time owned 6 Manor Street, now Barclays Bank, which was built by his father-in-law Thomas Brambles. Two of Mozley's sons, who would have holidayed at Bridlington, married sisters of Cardinal Newman.

THE
British Queen

COACH,

From Hull to Bridlington Quay,

Every Morning, at Half-past Six o'Clock.

By the way of Beverley to Brandsburton,

And arrives by the Sea Coast, at Bridlington Quay, about Twelve o'Clock.

The above Coach will leave *Bridlington Quay* every Morning, at Nine o'Clock, and arrive at *Hull* about Half-past Two; and when the Tide answers in the Afternoon, Passengers may go by way of *Burton* to *London,* or by the Steam Packet to *Gainsbro', Selby, Thorne,* or any other Conveyance up the Rivers.

☞ Passengers and Parcels booked at the Bull and Sun, and the George Inn, *Hull;* and at *George Chambers's,* the Sterling Castle, *Bridlington Quay.*

N. B. The Proprietors hope the above will meet with the approbation and support of the Public.

HULL, July 17, 1818.

Topping & Dawson, Printers, 47, Lowgate, Hull

Handbill advertising the British Queen Coach. *(East Riding of Yorkshire Council)* In 1828 the fares from Hull to Bridlington were 10s (50p) inside and 6s 6d (32½p) outside.

Early 19th-century milestone that formerly stood at Auburn alongside the coaching road long ago washed into the sea. *(Bayle Museum Trust)* There is another milestone in Cardigan Road outside Emmanuel Church.

kiss her. Bridlington had to be content with visits from the local aristocracy and in 1808 it was reported that the Duke and Duchess of Leeds, Marchioness and Lady Harriet Townsend, Earl and Countess Fitzwilliam, Viscount Milton, Earl Moira and Sir Thomas and Lady Vavasour were at the Quay.

The total number of visitors at any one time is unknown but there were 64 lodging houses in 1813 as well as the inns. This number had risen to 75 in 1823 and to 134 in 1846. Many of them were purpose built.

Travel to Bridlington was usually by coach or on horseback. The turnpiking of the main roads leading towards Bridlington from York, Hull and Beverley in the mid-18th century had improved access but the journey still could be hazardous. Rival coaches ran from Hull to Bridlington Quay in the early 1830s. The British Queen went on a scenic route via Brandesburton with 'the last six miles being close to the sea side', whilst the Magna Charta was advertised as taking the safe route via Driffield, 'the sea having made such dreadful havoc of the Brandesburton Road during the last few years as to render it dangerous travelling that way, being for five or six miles, quite at the edge of the cliff'.

Two visitors of more than local prominence who have left some account of their stay are Anna Seward, the 'Swan of Lichfield', and Charlotte Bronte. Both first saw the sea at Bridlington. In August 1793 after an enforced stay amongst the 'gay hurries of Scarborough' where she complained of the 'toilsome cliff … an inconvenience which we escape at Bridlington' Miss Seward reached her preferred 'quieter shore' at the Quay. She had particular praise for the 'boarded pier, one hundred and twenty yards in length, and on which nine people may walk abreast. There all the company of the place resort — and there the ocean gales rise on all sides around us, freely as we could taste them in a boat. Here we walk or sit, very often in the day, frequently when the huge billows are raging and lashing the pier on every side.'

Charlotte Bronte, accompanied by Ellen Nussey, paid her first visit to the seaside, at Bridlington, in September 1839. After staying at a farmhouse at nearby Easton the two friends spent

Promenading on the old wooden North Pier, Bridlington Quay by N. Whittock c. 1830. *(East Riding of Yorkshire Council)*

the last week of their holidays at Bridlington Quay in lodgings on Garrison Street near the Primitive Methodist Chapel (see p.49). The emotions Charlotte felt at the sight of the sea left her trembling and weeping but 'the evening parade on the Pier struck her as the greatest absurdity ... thither all the visitors seemed to assemble in such numbers that it was like a packed ball-room; people had to march round and round in regular file to secure any movement whatever'.

The late Georgian town

In the late Georgian period, in keeping with the national and local trend, there was a noticeable increase in the population and number of houses at Bridlington. Although partly explained by the rise of the resort, it is clear that Bridlington's role as a thriving market town also contributed to the increase in population and prosperity. The market held on a Saturday was said in 1823 to be 'plentifully supplied with all the necessaries, and as many of the luxuries of life, as the wants of the inhabitants require' and the corn market was 'well attended both by buyers and sellers'.

There was an expansion in trades and industries processing agricultural produce and manufacturing goods for the farming community, with the exception of maltsting, once the chief trade of Bridlington. In 1761 there had been 'upwards of sixty' malt kilns but by 1821 there were no more

Anna Seward (1742-1809). Largely unknown today, Anna Seward was a leading literary figure in her lifetime. A friend of Walter Scott and Robert Southey, her poems and her highly sentimental novel *Louisa* were greatly admired.

Cattle fair on Church Green,
Bridlington from T. Allen, *History
of the County of York*, 1829-31.
(East Riding of Yorkshire Council)
There were two annual fairs
held on the Church Green, on
the Monday before Whitsunday
and on 21 October, where the
trade was chiefly in horned
cattle, linen and woollen cloth
and toys.

than five, and these were only in partial use. John
Thompson attributed the decline to the poorer
quality barley grown following the enclosure of
the open fields in the area. Brewing continued
and there were five breweries in 1823. From the
animals brought to market fellmongers supplied
skins to the curriers and glovemakers and there
was a tannery on the site of Baptist Place. Soap
boiling, which was begun at Bridlington c. 1805,
required fat or oil, quick lime, potash and soda.

There were three hat manufactories with over
20 employees, in addition to the women
outworkers 'cutting skins, carding wool, and lin-
ing and preparing the hats for sale'. There were
also up to a dozen women making straw hats. A
limited textile industry is apparent from the occasional references to flaxdressers, dyers, weavers
and linen and worsted manufactories. At the
Quay two industries linked to the port, shipbuilding and ropemaking, flourished during the Napoleonic wars but were in decline by the 1820s.

Population and Houses, 1801-41.

Year	Population	Houses
1801	3,130	707
1811	3,741	869
1821	4,275	953
1831	4,792	1,081
1841	5,162	1,219

The coming of the railway

Early in 1834 a meeting was held at the Bayle, under the chairmanship of the Chief Lord, to consider the building of a 'Rail-Road from the Quay to the West Riding'. A committee was soon after established and a report published which envisaged that more than half the income would come from transporting fish, with sheep, wool and fat cattle being next in importance. Passenger traffic was thought to be of minimal importance.

Nothing came of this scheme, and it was not until eleven years later, on 30 June 1845, that Royal Assent was given to an Act authorising a 'Branch Railway from and out of the Main Line' of the Hull and Selby Railway 'at or near a place called Dairy Cotes' to Bridlington where it was to 'terminate at or near a certain place called the Gravel Pits (Midway Green)'. There was a suggestion that the line terminate at the Quay near Prospect Street, but the residents of the Old Town successfully petitioned for the station to be midway between the two settlements because 'Bridlington is the ancient and parent town of the parish and where the bulk of the inhabitants reside. The Quay is only an Hamlet'.

The line, built with impressive speed, was opened with great ceremony on 6 October 1846 with three locomotives and 66 railway carriages travelling from Hull. In the morning the chief inhabitants of Bridlington assembled at the Market Place and processed to the new railway station. Two bands of music accompanied the procession that was led by a banner bearing the Royal Arms and was punctuated by other banners with other slogans. When the first train arrived from Hull just after 1.00 p.m. it was greeted by 'several rounds of applause'. A sumptuous luncheon was provided in the Station goods shed, presided over by the 'Railway King' George Hudson who was presented with a congratulatory address by the Lords Feoffees. In reply Hudson declared his hope that the railway 'would be the means of extending the commerce of that district and above all that it would be the means of conveying thousands to that place so that its invigorating breezes might confer on them renewed health.' At 3.30 p.m. the visitors returned to Hull for a banquet but at Bridlington the momentous day ended with a firework display.

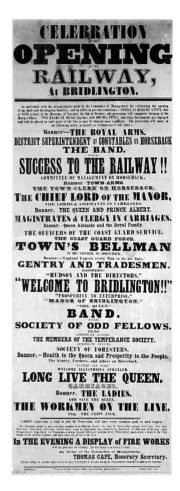

Poster advertising the opening ceremony for the Hull-Bridlington Railway. *(Bayle Museum Trust)*

A rare view of Bridlington Station c. 1880 showing the handsome Tuscan portico which was removed in 1892. *(F.F. Johnson)* The station was designed by G.T. Andrews. The present station was added to the east in 1912.

Excursion poster June 1848. *(Bayle Museum Trust)* In 1847 the *Hull Advertiser* praised the railways for running cheap excursion trains which 'are rendering the country inestimable service, by popularising enjoyments which have been hitherto restricted to a class'.

Just over a year later, with the opening of the Bridlington-Filey line on 18 October 1847, the resort was linked to the York to Scarborough railway line. A more direct route to the West Riding was secured when the Market Weighton to Driffield line was opened on 1 May 1890.

The promoters of the Hull to Bridlington line had, unlike their predecessors eleven years before, realised that passenger traffic was going to be of prime importance and with the railway came the excursion train and day tripper, transforming the genteel resort. Typical of the new visitors were those on a firm's outing or the annual Sunday School treat. In June 1847 622 Sunday School children from Beverley and 98 teachers filled 35 carriages on a special train to Bridlington.

Origins of the visitors

'Bridlington attracts numbers of that class of visitors for whom Hornsea is too quiet and Scarborough too gay.'

Walter White, *A Month in Yorkshire*, 1858.

The opening of the railway not only brought more visitors to Bridlington but they came from further afield. The great majority still came from Yorkshire. In one week in July 1843 66% of the visitors recorded came from Yorkshire, 29% from Lincolnshire, Nottinghamshire and Derbyshire and 5% from the rest of Britain. In 1850 the percentages were much the same but there was a marked increase from 31% to 42% coming from the West Riding. This pattern continued with 53% coming from the West Riding in 1866 and 57% in 1880. The percentages from the rest of Yorkshire and the North East Midlands dropped accordingly, but those coming from Hull stayed consistently around 14.5%. Bridlington was truly 'Leeds-plus-Hull-cum Sheffield super Mare' as one journalist referred to the resort in 1889.

The information on visitors comes from the weekly lists that were published in the local papers throughout the season. Bridlington usually had two or three newspapers and it was the sales in the summer to visitors, eager to see who was staying in the town and where, that kept the papers going all year. There was a particular interest in spotting titled visitors, or leading dignitaries from your home town.

Victoria Rooms

On the eve of the arrival of the railway the 'sources of amusement' at Bridlington were still, as in 1821, 'rather circumscribed' and consisted of little more than promenading, riding and sailing. In preparation for the expected increase in visitors with the opening of the railway a group of townspeople formed the Bridlington Quay Public

The *Bridlington Free Press* Office, 54 High Street, 1895. First published in January 1859 when there were two other newspapers in the town; the *Bridlington Quay Mercury* (1850-68) and the *Bridlington Quay Observer* (1857-99); it has outlived them and its later rivals the *Bridlington and Quay Gazette* (1874-1914) and the *Bridlington and Quay Chronicle* (1897-1954). The first Bridlington newspapers, both short lived, were published in 1843.

THE BRIDLINGTON-QUAY MERCURY.

LIST OF VISITORS.

The utility of a List of Visitors can only be proportionate to its correctness; therefore we will feel obliged if parties observing inaccuracies will give notice to the Collector, or at the Publishing-office, Queen-street, Bridlington-Quay, in order that they may be remedied in our succeeding number.

Part of the visitors' list from *The Bridlington-Quay Mercury, General Advertiser and Weekly List of Visitors* for 8 August 1850.

Victoria Rooms, Bridlington Quay. Drawing by the architect Samuel Worth of Sheffield, 1846. *(East Riding of Yorkshire Council)* Its rooms were later used for many purposes including cinematograph shows and it housed an early amusement arcade. Little more than a year after the Borough Council had ceased using the building for their meetings it was destroyed by fire on 22 September 1933.

Playbill for a performance at the Victoria Rooms, September 1863. *(East Riding of Yorkshire Council)*

Rooms Association in September 1845. Its object was to purchase 'a suitable site, and to erect an ornamental building which will include a News-Room, a Promenade Room, and other Rooms adapted for general purposes'. The site chosen was at the landward end of the North Pier and after several delays, caused by objections from the Harbour Commissioners, the public rooms were finally built late in 1847.

The Victoria Rooms, as they became known, remained for almost 50 years the resort's prime location for most cultural and social events in both summer and winter. Lectures, concerts, theatrical performances, and a host of public meetings were held there. Under the management of 'Professor' J.M. Wilson (1826-98), best remembered as the conductor of the Parade band, the musical events ranged from visits by Mr Joe Brown 'late of the Christy Minstrels' to Christmas performances of the Messiah.

The rooms were purchased by the Local Board in 1879. In 1893 they became, in part, the Town Hall when the board meetings were transferred there from 45 High Street.

The Local Board

The hoped for prosperity heralded by the opening of the railway did not materialise. One resident claimed that the event robbed the port of its coal trade and rendered the Quay 'in winter, a dismal and dispirited town'. After an initial rise the population of Bridlington decreased in the years 1851-61. The lack of facilities, both in the way of accommodation and entertainments, and the serious erosion of the cliffs to the north of the harbour, all contributed to deter the visitor. Matters rapidly improved following the adoption of the 1858 Local Government Act in 1863 and the establishment of a Local Board to run the affairs of Bridlington.

The nine elected as members of the first board included Thomas Harland, solicitor, Edward Harding, banker, Mark Cooper, chemist, Dr C.F. Hutchinson, Joseph Beauvais. linen draper, Thomas Cape, grocer and Thomas Prickett who was chosen as chairman. Cape, Harding and Prickett were also Lords Feoffees. Charles Gray was the clerk to the board throughout its existence 1863-94.

The board had its first meeting in June at the Corn Exchange and by September they had engaged a civil engineer to supply plans for the improvement of the town. The priority was the construction of a sea wall to the north of the harbour. A rate was levied, not without opposition, and a loan obtained. The new sea wall with the parade behind was opened to the public on 17 June 1867. The 'charming marine promenade' was nearly 700 feet (214 m.) long and was described ten years later as being 'beautifully laid out with flower beds, shrubberies, and walks; it has also several commodious summer-houses in various parts of the grounds, where visitors may seek shelter from sun and rain, and yet enjoy the surrounding scene. In the centre of the grounds is a spacious Pavilion, where an excellent Band performs twice a day during the season.'

Building the Sea Wall Parade 1866-7. *(East Riding of Yorkshire Council)* The view from the roof of the Victoria Rooms. In the far distance can be seen the recently built Alexandra Hotel, towards the middle is Fort Hall, and in the foreground is the Primitive Methodist Chapel of 1833. This is the Ranters' Chapel from which Charlotte Bronte heard intriguing sounds when in lodgings nearby in 1839.

Bridlington, Hilderthorpe and Sewerby: population 1841-1891.

Year	1841	1851	1861	1871	1881	1891
Bridlington & Quay	5,162	5,839	5,775	6,203	6,642	6,840
Hilderthorpe	116	147	176	715	1475	1,752
Sewerby & Marton	352	356	342	452	547	628
Total population	5,630	6,342	6,293	7,370	8,664	9,220

Prince's Parade in the 1880s. *(Bayle Museum Trust)* The Sea Wall Parade was re-named the Prince's Parade in July 1888 in honour of the visit of Prince Albert Victor, son of the Prince of Wales. In 1890 the Local Board arranged for the Prince's Parade to be illuminated by electricity.

Following the completion of the Sea Wall Parade the Local Board went ahead with providing further defences and a promenade along the sea front. The wooden Victoria Sea Defences were built by the board in 1869-70, followed by the Alexandra Sea Wall, north of Sands (Trinity) Cut, in 1879-81, and, after much protest and a petition from 120 residents of Sheffield, the Beaconsfield Sea Wall was constructed in 1888. Including the defences provided by private developers, the whole length of the sea front to the north of the harbour, in and beyond the board's area, was protected by the 1890s.

Many of the board's meetings were stormy, with a vocal faction opposing expenditure on public schemes. Members walked out of meetings and there were frequent resignations of chairmen and others. The local press had much to report. Nevertheless in its 31 years of existence the board laid the foundations for the expansion and prosperity of the later 1890s. Of particular importance was the drainage scheme first considered in the early 1870s but not completed until 1885. The board also oversaw the rapid development of the town, requiring any plans for new buildings or alterations to be submitted for approval.

Accommodating the visitors

For twenty years after the coming of the railway the Britannia Inn on Prince Street remained the chief place to stay at the Quay. It was largely rebuilt at this time but its setting, hemmed in between the harbour and the busiest commercial street and with no grounds, meant that its days were numbered. Then in 1866 Mark Barr built the Alexandra Hotel on Sewerby Terrace. This impressive building, designed by the Scarborough architect W.B. Stewart, and set in three acres of gardens, was said on opening to contain 120 rooms, and to be 'one of the most beautiful of modern structures to be found in any of the sea-bathing places on the east coast'.

By the 1860s Bridlington was no longer the resort of the gentry and aristocracy. The clientele of the newly-built Alexandra were more likely to be from the rising Victorian middle class — the families of merchants, tradesmen and professionals. Amongst those staying at the hotel in June 1868 were the wealthy Hull shipowner Thomas Wilson and family from Park House, Cottingham, and the Hull banker Edmund Smith and family from Ferriby Manor, North Ferriby.

Bridlington's handful of inns only accommodated a small number of the visitors. The list of visitors in the *Mercury* 8 August 1850 records 612 people plus un-named children and servants staying in 166 lodging houses and only 58 staying at

The Britannia Hotel, Prince Street 1897. *(East Riding of Yorkshire Council)* A late 18th-century building much altered in the 19th century. It was destroyed in a German bombing raid in August 1940. The block of buildings including the Tourist Information Centre stand on the site.

Belle Vue Terrace, Tennyson Avenue. Built c. 1840-2. The least altered of the terraces to have survived from before the coming of the railway.

Marlborough Terrace c. 1890. *(Martin Craven)* It was built c. 1870.

The Alexandra Hotel in the 1890s. *(Martin Craven)* In 1920 the hotel frontage was nearly trebled in size providing over 200 bedrooms and a fine ballroom. Bridlington's grandest hotel closed in 1975. It was demolished soon after and a block of luxury flats erected on its site.

the six inns. By 1892 there were around 420 lodging houses listed at the Quay and Hilderthorpe and 23 hotels. There were many other residents who took in lodgers during the season.

In the second half of the 19th century the greater part of the new buildings erected at the Quay were designed to accommodate visitors. Amongst the earliest and the grandest were the developments along the sea front immediately to the north of Prince Street. Here on the initiative of the Local Board an area of earlier 19th-century housing forming part of Cliff Street, Cliff Square and part of Garrison Street was cleared in 1866-7 and a new street (Marlborough Terrace) laid out. The land was bought by G.W. Travis of Sheffield, who settled in Bridlington in 1869. He brought with him Joseph Earnshaw who became the architect of Victorian Bridlington. For Travis Earnshaw designed Marlborough Terrace and the Crescent, both built 1869-71, and also Albion Terrace (1878) and Royal Crescent on the Beaconsfield Estate further north. He laid out Wellington Road and also in the late 1870s some of the earliest streets on the south side in Hilderthorpe.

By 1888 there were some 350 households in Hilderthorpe. Of the streets here West Street had 63 houses of which only seven, including a police station, two shops and a herring curer's, were not listed as lodging houses. Similarly the fourteen houses in Bow Street and ten of the seventeen houses in Ferndale Terrace were occupied by lodging house keepers. The best lodgings were to be found in Pembroke Terrace, built in the late 1870s and in Railway (later Windsor) Crescent. On the east side of the latter ran a short-lived railway line from the station to the harbour. It was disused by 1866 but its route determined the layout of the street.

The market town

The seaside resort at the Quay so dominates the history of Bridlington from the mid-19th century that the Old Town's continuing role as a market town gets forgotten. Until the 1890s the majority of the population of Bridlington lived in the Old Town and their economy was closely linked with that of the local farming community. The two fairs, at Whitsun and in October, and the November statute hirings were the high points of

Helter Skelter at Bridlington Fair.
(Lords Feoffees) The October
Pleasure Fair on High Green.
It remained there until 1973
when it was moved to
Hilderthorpe Road.

Elevation of Bridlington Police
Station and Lock-up by H.F.
Lockwood 1843. *(East Riding of
Yorkshire Archives and Records
Service)* Similar to others built
at Driffield, Howden and Market
Weighton except for its
distinctive Egyptian style
windows with sloping sides.
The building closed in 1881.

the calendar. At the Martinmas hirings hundreds
of farm servants, men and women, would be hired
for the year and would also spend much of their
year's wages on clothes and entertainments. The
hirings were riotous occasions. In 1872 an edito-
rial in the Bridlington Free Press described them
as 'this annual evil ... this barbarous and soul
endangering system'.

A quieter affair was the weekly Saturday market when the west end of the High Street and the
Market Place were packed with stalls and carriers'
carts. In 1858 some 40 carriers from 26 villages
regularly went to Bridlington on market day, and
many on a Wednesday as well. They came from as
far afield as Filey, Wold Newton, Langtoft, Driffield and Beeford; a radius of about ten miles. The
market was administered by the Lords Feoffees
and Assistants of the Manor of Bridlington, the
oldest of the numerous local government bodies
that existed in the Victorian town.

Bridlington, as the local market town, was the
obvious location for the central workhouse when
the new Poor Law Union was established in 1836.
The workhouse built on Marton Road in 1847-8
became the administrative centre for the care of
the poor for 32 townships stretching from Hunmanby in the north to Skipsea in the south and
Thwing in the west. The area of the Bridlington
Poor Law Union was also the area for the Bridlington Rural District in 1894-1974. The Old
Town was the centre for the Dickering Petty
Sessions Division with the magistrates meeting
every Saturday in a room in the yard of the Black
Lion Inn. The County Court met in the same
room monthly. The police station and lock-up
for the division was built on Nungate (Sewerby
Road) in 1843-4.

To these wider administrative units were added
those confined to the township; the Local Board
and Urban Sanitary Authority in 1863, the Burial
Board in 1873, and the School Board in 1879. The

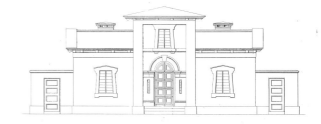

Burial Board established the cemetery on Sewerby Road. Its Gothic chapels, linked by an archway topped by a tall spire, are dated 1879. Other services were provided by the Burlington Gas Light Company, formed 1836, which took over gasworks established on Quay Road in 1833, and the Bridlington and Quay Water Company set up in 1865 with a reservoir and pumping station at the junction of Mill Lane and Marton Road.

Education and self-help were much promoted in Victorian Bridlington. As well as having the near defunct Grammar School (closed 1866) and the Knitting School (closed 1872), the Old Town had a National School established in 1818. This was a church school run by the local branch of the National Society for Promoting the Education of the Poor in the Principles of the Church of England. A new school was built on North Back Lane in 1826 and an infants' school on Church Green in 1857. At the Quay the National School established on Quay Road in 1850 was taken over by the school board in 1879 and became Quay Girls' School. A second board school was built in West Street, Hilderthorpe in 1882. There was also a Wesleyan day school at the Quay adjoining the chapel by 1840.

Self-help and improvement were the objectives of numerous friendly societies, two temperance

The banner of the Bridlington Amicable Society. *(East Riding of Yorkshire Council)* This friendly society, founded in 1848, had over 150 members in the 1870s-80s.

The Lloyd Hospital, Quay Road. *(East Riding of Yorkshire Council)* Another of Bridlington's Victorian institutions. It was founded in 1868 by Alicia Lloyd, sister of Yarburgh Lloyd Greame of Sewerby. The purpose-built hospital designed by Smith and Brodrick was opened in 1876. It was demolished in the 1990s.

societies, a mechanics' institute and a mutual improvement society. The Victorian town abounded with other organisations including cricket, cycling, football and lawn tennis clubs, as well as the Bridlington Agricultural Society established in 1835, and the Floral and Horticultural Society, both of which had annual shows. The Victoria Sailors' and Working Men's Club was founded in 1865 and the Literary and Debating Society in 1898.

Church and chapel

Attending a church or chapel at the resort was as much a part of the holiday as a walk along the Prince's Parade. Bridlington offered plenty of choice as there were fifteen places of worship in the town in 1888.

On Sunday 30 March 1851 a national census of religious worship was undertaken alongside the decennial census of population. At a time when the population of the town was approaching 6000 the total number recorded attending services in Bridlington and Bridlington Quay on that day was 4029. This would include many people who went to more than one service. Of the numbers attending 1538 (38%) went to one or other of the Anglican churches and 2491 (62%) to the six Nonconformist chapels.

In 1851 the Anglican churches were the Priory Church and Christ Church on Quay Road. The Church of England had lagged behind the Nonconformists in providing a place of worship at the Quay and, until the building of Christ Church in 1841, visitors and residents had to make the long journey to the Priory on a Sunday. Christ Church was built on land donated by John Rickaby. A second Anglican church at the Quay, Holy Trinity, was built at the top of Promenade in 1871, chiefly paid for by the Revd Yarburgh Lloyd Greame of Sewerby. Two years earlier Captain Barnes had built the temporary church of St Anne on Flamborough Road. It caused much controversy as its services were markedly High Church in contrast to the strong Evangelical tradition of worship at the Priory and Christ Church. After St Anne's Convalescent Home was built by Captain Barnes the iron church was re-erected alongside. It was replaced in 1897 by a brick chapel to which a chancel was added in 1909. An Anglican mission

Holy Trinity, Promenade. *(Lords Feoffees)* Designed by the Hull architect R.G. Smith, who came from Marton, its tall spire soon became a landmark in the town.

church, St Hilda, was built on Thorpe Street in 1874 to serve the growing community in Hilderthorpe. It was in Christ Church parish as was its replacement Emmanuel Church, Cardigan Road, which opened in 1903. Emmanuel Church was completed in 1928 and destroyed by fire in August 1995.

In all the activity of opening new churches the Priory Church of St Mary was not forgotten and it underwent extensive restoration, in several phases, between the years 1846 and 1884. In the 1840s the great west window was restored and part of the roof renewed under the direction of Edmund Sharpe. In 1855-8 the church was re-pewed and the rest of the roof replaced. Sir George Gilbert Scott added upper storeys to both of the western towers, giving the church its familiar outline, in 1875-6 and in 1884 he restored the north porch.

Christ Church, Quay Road. *(East Riding of Yorkshire Council)* One of the early works of Sir George Gilbert Scott. The church was enlarged in 1851 and the spire added in 1859.

Attendances at Methodist chapels exceeded those at the Anglican churches in 1851, even if the Sunday scholars (who were most numerous at the Priory where it was a requirement that the pupils at the National School attend services) are included in the figures. There were four Methodist chapels; two Wesleyan and two Primitive Methodist. Primitive Methodism arrived at Bridlington in 1819 and by the first visit of William Clowes in January 1821 there were 50 members. Chapels were built at the Old Town and the Quay in 1833. A fifth Methodist chapel was built on Promenade in 1852 for the Wesleyan Reformers, following a split in the movement that initially had a serious impact on the Bridlington Wesleyan Circuit.

Methodism, with its emphasis on activities throughout the week, dominated the lives of many in the town. Able ministers were appointed to Bridlington, including Rudyard Kipling's grandfather in 1844, and celebrated preachers visited in the summer months when the chapels were full to overflowing. Many of the leading townspeople were 'chapel' rather than 'church' and they subscribed handsomely to the rebuilding funds.

St John's Burlington Methodist Church from a drawing by the architect Joseph Earnshaw. *(East Riding of Yorkshire Council)*

The strength and confidence of Nonconformity in later Victorian Bridlington is amply demonstrated by a catalogue of the chapels that were erected around the town in the 1870s-80s. It is an impressive list.

1870   Primitive Methodist, Chapel Street (rebuilt 1879)
1872   United Methodist Free Church, Promenade
1873   Wesleyan Methodist (Quay), Chapel Street
1874   Baptist, Quay Road
1877   Primitive Methodist, St John Street
1879   Congregational (Trinity), Promenade
1879   Primitive Methodist (Central), Chapel Street
1884   Wesleyan Methodist (St John's Burlington), St John Street

Baptist Church, Quay Road. *(East Riding of Yorkshire Council)* Built 1874 to the designs of Samuel Musgrave of Hull. It replaced the chapel in Baylegate. It was demolished in 1985 leaving only the later schoolroom for services.

In 1886 the Salvation Army took over the former Temperance Hall in Wellington Road and the Congregational church on St John Street was restored. The latter was demolished for road widening and a new church built on the corner of Brett Street in 1906. The influx of residents from West Riding towns helped revive the fortunes of the older denominations, the Baptists and Congregationalists, and the re-establishment of a Quaker Meeting House in Havelock Street in 1903.

The small Roman Catholic community did not have a resident priest at Bridlington before 1868. The first Roman Catholic church, an iron building dedicated to St William on Wellington Road, was opened in 1886 and replaced by the present church in 1893-4.

The harbour

Thanks to the actions of the Harbour Commissioners appointed under the act of 1837, and the interest shown by the chairman Arthur Strickland of King Street, the rebuilding of the North and South Piers was completed in 1848. It was hoped that the harbour would benefit from the recent opening of the railway. But this was not the case as the railway, rather than bringing trade to the port, did the opposite. The quantity of corn exported dropped from 37,700 quarters in 1841 to only 1,000 quarters in 1856-7. The numbers of ships entering the harbour 'for trade' decreased from 111 in 1849 to 82 in 1855.

Nationally the spread of the railways hit the coastal trade, including the carriage of coal from the north-east ports. The coble owners of Bridlington had made much of their living by carrying provisions to the passing fleets of colliers and the hundreds of sailing ships that at times took shelter in Bridlington Bay. Necessity drove the coble

Herring auction on Gummer's Wharf, Bridlington c. 1900. *(East Riding of Yorkshire Council).* Herrings had been landed at Bridlington Quay since the middle ages. At the end of the 19th century the harbour was a base for the Scottish herring industry. In October 1899 there were upwards of 30 boats at Bridlington belonging to Banff, Inverness and other ports and 'lasses' from Aberdeen were busy gutting herrings.

owners to turn to trawling and thereby contribute to the founding of the Bridlington fishing industry

Offshore trawling had first taken place off the Yorkshire coast in 1819 when Colonel Ralph Creyke of Marton Hall experimented with a Bridlington-registered boat. There were no further developments locally until mid-century. The fishing communities of Flamborough, Filey and further north would not contemplate trawling but at Bridlington, where there was no established fishing community, there was no such opposition. In 1891 there were more than 100 fishermen living at Bridlington Quay, four times as many as in 1851. Some, such as the Newbys, had come from East Anglian ports. By 1902 there were 84 fishing boats belonging to Bridlington.

The harbour has always been one of the greatest attractions of Bridlington for the visitor. The late 18th-century gentry visitors enjoyed promenading on the North Pier and the more adventurous would take a sail in a 'cleaned' coble. 'Trips round the bay' became an important additional source of income for coble owners at the Quay. By the mid-19th century longer excursions were provided by paddle steamers, the earliest coming down the coast from Scarborough. In the 1840s it cost 2s 6d (12.5p) for a trip from

Bridlington Harbour with paddle steamer, 1854. *(Bayle Museum Trust)*

Revd Henry F. Barnes, vicar of Bridlington. *(East Riding of Yorkshitre Council)* Founder of the Association for the Protection of Sea Birds. The actions of the Association led to the passing of the Sea Birds Preservation Act in 1869.

Bridlington to Scarborough on the *United Kingdom,* with an 'excellent quadrille band' in attendance.

In July 1876 a visitor from Essex noted in his diary: 'Went on the pier again — a busy scene — saw a great many pleasure boats going in and out — and a steamer arrived — the *Friend* — evidently a steam tug turned into a passenger boat for the time. She went out for an hour or two's steam past the head.'

The 'head', Flamborough Head, with its dramatic scenery and its 'inconceivable number of sea-fowl', has always been the most popular destination. Unfortunately it became common from the 1840s for visitors to go out in boats for the purpose of shooting sea birds for 'sport'. Thousands of the birds were slaughtered and many 'wounded and bleeding, were left to die a lingering and agonising death in the waters'. When a speaker at a meeting of the British Association for the Advancement of Science in 1868 denounced the people of Bridlington for their atrocious cruelty to sea birds the vicar, the Revd Henry Barnes (later Barnes-Lawrence) leapt to their defence. At a meeting at Bridlington Vicarage on 21 October 1868 the Association for the Protection of Sea Birds was founded.

Bridlington's lifeboats

Bridlington Bay, protected to the north by the cliffs of Flamborough Head, is a place of refuge for shipping when gales are blowing from the north or west and in the mid-19th century as many as 600 sailing vessels could be found sheltering in the bay at any one time.

When gales blow from the south and east the bay can become a death trap and in the years 1770-1806 at least 174 ships were lost in the bay and around Flamborough Head. A subscription was raised and a lifeboat acquired for Bridlington in 1805 and the next year Benjamin Milne, the Collector of Customs at Bridlington, persuaded Trinity House to build the lighthouse on Flamborough Head.

On the founding of the Royal National Lifeboat Institution (R.N.L.I.) in 1824 a new lifeboat was presented to Bridlington. It served for 41 years during which time at least 82 lives were saved. The successor boat, the *Robert Whitworth*

was objected to by the fisherman and in 1866 Count Batthyany, a Hungarian nobleman who lived for a time on Promenade, presented them with a boat, the *Harbinger,* built to their own specifications by David Purdon of Bridlington.

Following the 'Great Gale' of 1871, Bridlington was provided with a third lifeboat, the *Seagull* presented to the sailors of the town by the Revd Yarburgh Lloyd-Greame of Sewerby. Competition was rife between the lifeboats and in 1886, when all three went to help a stranded brigantine, the *Harbinger* was so badly battered that it was withdrawn from service. Likewise in March 1898 the *Seagull,* which was managed by the Sailors' and Working Men's Club, and the R.N.L.I. boat the *William John and Frances,* were wrecked when attempting to help the brigantine *Lucinda.*

In the 20th century a succession of seven R.N.L.I. lifeboats served Bridlington during which time almost 300 lives were saved. More lives than this have been saved by the inshore lifeboats that were first introduced in 1966. The inshore lifeboat is provided by the Lords Feoffees after whom it is named.

The *Seagull* after it had been wrecked in 1898. *(F.F. Johnson)* It was placed on show at the end of Fort Terrace to raise funds for the families of the drowned men.

The 'Great Gale' of February 1871

Bridlington Bay has been hit by many storms over the centuries, with considerable loss of life, but the gale that took place on Friday 10 February

1871 has become legendary. The 'Great Gale' is remembered because of the number of ships involved and the numbers drowned, particularly the local lifeboatmen. The most dramatic and harrowing scenes took place directly in front of the harbour and the north and south shore, watched helplessly by hundreds of spectators throughout the day. The sight and cries of drowning sailors and the wreckage strewn along the sands had a great impact on the town. At least 70 were drowned in the bay and 30 ships were wrecked.

The two Bridlington lifeboats, the R.N.L.I. boat the *Robert Whitworth* and the fishermen's boat the *Harbinger,* put to sea and saved many lives. After rescuing the crews of three ships the *Harbinger* was launched again around noon and brought safely to the shore the crew of a brig. The boat then went out to another stranded brig — the *Delta* of Whitby. During a vain attempt to rescue the lone survivor on this ship the lifeboat was overturned and six of the nine crew were drowned, including Purdon.

Four days after the storm, on 14 February, a most impressive funeral of 23 of the drowned sailors took place at the Priory. A huge procession watched by over 4,000 people slowly progressed

The Great Gale 1871 by J.T.Allerston. *(Harbour Commissioners)* It shows the brig *Delta* and the overturned lifeboat *Harbinger.*

from the Quay to the Old Town. A monument was erected in the churchyard and each February a memorial service is held in Bridlington Priory for those lost in the Great Gale of 1871.

The late Victorian and Edwardian resort

The 25 years before the First World War was the high point for the English seaside resort. Bridlington was no exception. The population of the town rose from 9,220 in 1891 (including Hilderthorpe and Sewerby and Marton) to 14,334 for the borough in 1911. Throughout the season thousands were pouring in daily by train. The number of tickets collected at Bridlington station in 1896 was 314,484 of which the highest monthly figures were in July (79,374) and August (78,497). By comparison the number of tickets collected at Scarborough was 850,277, at Redcar 385,813, at Hornsea 117,594, at Withernsea 95,348 and at Filey 82,975.

Many of the visitors were trippers and this was not to everyone's liking. In 1896 a Wiltshire clergyman on holiday in Bridlington complained in his parish magazine that the resort was overrun, two or three times a week, with trippers from Sheffield, Leeds, York and Hull 'some of whom are of the rougher sort'. Large numbers came from West Riding towns just for an evening at the seaside, either to stroll along the pier or terraces or to go to a show. Many did stay for a week or more and are still recorded in visitors' lists up to the First World War. On 2 August 1901 the list of visitors in the *Free Press* records 4959 people, plus children and servants, staying in 955 apartments, 224 in twelve boarding houses and 218 in nine hotels. It was reported in 1912 that the resident population was 15,000 but the sleeping population during the height of the season was nearly 60,000.

The term 'apartment' had taken the place of lodging house by 1901. The mass of visitors to Bridlington up to the Second World War, and beyond stayed not in hotels or even boarding houses but in 'apartments'. Here the holidaymakers paid only for the rooms. They bought their own food and the landlady cooked it and charged for 'the cruet'. Apartments ranged from the 'superior' in the many-roomed purpose-built lodging

THE SCARBOROUGH

EXPRESS

FRIDAY EVENING, Feb. 17th,

WITH SUPPLEMENT (GRATIS,)

Will contain a FULL REPORT of the

Dreadful Shipwrecks

At BRIDLINGTON QUAY and on the Coast.

THE

Interment of 23 bodies

ON TUESDAY LAST.

Public Procession.

Presentation of a New Lifeboat Suitable to the locality.

Meeting for Relief of Widows & Orphans.

Meeting of the Sailors and Boatmen.

The "EXPRESS" contains the longest and most graphic description of the above calamity yet published.

Sold by Mr. G. FURBY, Bridlington Quay, and Mr. W. HESELTON, Bridlington.

Flyer for the *Scarborough Express* report on the Great Gale, 17 February 1871. *(East Riding of Yorkshire Council)*

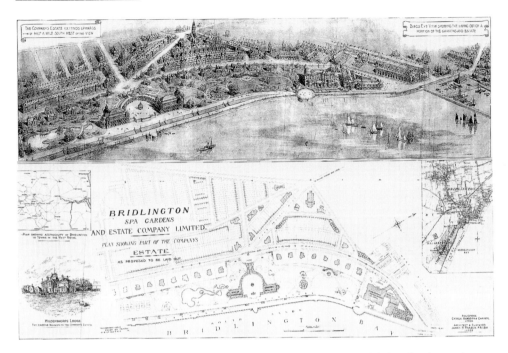

Bridlington Spa Gardens, 1895. An ambitious scheme not followed by Whitaker Brothers when they developed the land from 1896.

Norwegian Villas, South Cliff. *(Norman Creaser)* Whitakers erected five wooden Norwegian villas on their estate in 1898 providing Bridlington with one of its more original examples of seaside architecture.

houses on the front to the best bedroom let out for the season in the fisherman's terraced cottage in a back street near the harbour. By 1901 2,101 (42%) of the visitors were staying in Hilderthorpe; 50 years earlier there had been none.

Hilderthorpe, where the population rose from less than 150 in 1861 to 3,053 in 1911, was transformed with the development of middle class housing after 1900. There had been plans for a villa estate, Albert Town, in Hilderthorpe in 1866, but it had come to nothing; as had Colonel Rhodes' scheme for South Burlington in 1875, and the ambitious proposals for Bridlington Spa Gardens of 1895. Elements of the last scheme were, however, adopted by Whitaker Brothers of Horsforth, Leeds when they bought the land the following year. As well as building the Spa (see below) Whitakers laid out a middle-class estate on Belgrave Road, Cardigan Road, Horsforth Avenue and Roundhay Road 1896-1900. These were residential streets of detached or semi-detached houses set back in gardens. Many of the houses were occupied by the families of men who worked in Hull or Leeds and travelled daily by rail in specially designed club saloons. A number of the houses had tennis courts. By 1921 there were over 2,800 Bridlington residents who worked in Hull or the West Riding.

Edwardian suburbia, Cardigan Road, Bridlington, 1998. The street was laid out in 1899 and plans for the first house were submitted by Whitakers in November that year. By 1911 there were 36 houses on Cardigan Road and the householders included a number of Hull businessmen: a solicitor, chairmen or family members of leading firms of printers, brassfounders and oil refiners, and the Hull Stipendiary Magistrate.

The Spa Theatre and Opera House, built 1907. *(East Riding of Yorkshire Council)* The original theatre was destroyed by fire in October 1906. It was replaced by this much grander building the following year.

Palaces of pleasure

The need for new places of entertainment was the constant cry of the Bridlington press in the 1880s and early 1890s. There had been proposals for a seaside pier, and four companies were formed for this purpose in the years 1879-99, but these came to nothing. A wooden Switchback Railway was erected in a field north of Sands Lane by 1890 and was popular for some years. It closed in 1912.

What was needed was a hall or rooms where concerts, plays and balls could be held as a change from what one journalist described as the 'everlasting fireworks' provided on the Royal Prince's Parade. There was an admission charge for the Parade so that 'the better class of visitors, who usually stayed for several months at a time' could have 'a secluded place where they could get away from the rough excursionists'.

In 1896, almost 50 years after the opening of the Victoria Rooms, the resort was provided with not one but two new 'pleasure domes' — the People's Palace, Quay Road, and the New Spa and Gardens. The People's Palace was built for William Holmes of Leeds on the grounds of a former villa, Rosendale. It comprised a large concert hall, to seat 1,500, with a dance hall below, a 'spacious' refreshment room and two large dining rooms. Renamed the Hippodrome when it became a cinema in 1911, it closed after bomb damage in 1940. The entrance with flanking shops was demolished 1996. The New Spa and Gardens were part of the development of the South Bridlington estate by the Whitaker Brothers of Horsforth, Leeds. Five acres were laid out with grassy slopes, flower beds and walks, and a lake, and a theatre and concert hall, band stand and refreshment rooms were built.

The opening of the Spa clearly hit the Prince's Parade but, other than rebuilding the bandstand, little action was taken by the Corporation until 1904, when the glass and iron Floral Pavilion was constructed alongside the bandstand. Two years later they built the Grand Pavilion on the site of the fort at the north end of the Prince's Parade. Capable of seating 2,000, it was a large wooden building with an Oriental appearance. It was typical of the 'end of pier' pavilions found at many seaside resorts. The other attractions of the Parade included the Floral Clock (from 1907), the

The New Spa c. 1896.
(East Riding of Yorkshire Council)
Two years later a glass 'dome'
was constructed and a band
engaged for the season. At night
the gardens were illuminated by
hundreds of different-coloured
electric lights. During its first
month the Spa had 80,000
visitors.

The Grand Pavilion, 1906. *(East
Riding of Yorkshire Council)*

Floral Staircase, the Floral Carpet, and a 'topiary'
Bear. On gala nights there were often fireworks
and the Parade was illuminated by thousands of
fairy lamps and Chinese lanterns.

Moving pictures arrived at Bridlington by 1906
when the Corporation engaged The Loyal
Dominion Animated Picture Company to show
cinematograph films at the Grand Pavilion. Soon
everywhere was into the craze. Early in 1909 films
were being shown at the New Spa Opera House,
and later that same year the Corporation

The Floral Pavilion and
Bandstand, c. 1908.
(East Riding of Yorkshire Council)

purchased a 'Bioscope machine' to show films at
the Victoria Rooms. The People's Palace followed
in 1910 and Field's Oriental Lounge in 1912.

The first dedicated picture palace was the old
Victorian Temperance Hall on Quay Road which
was transformed to the Picturedrome (the Roxy
from the mid-1930s) in 1912, with an impressive
faience façade by the Hull cinema architect
H.P. Binks.

The beach

In answer to a survey in the 1980s holidaymakers overwhelming declared that what they liked
most about Bridlington was the beach. It was
much the same a hundred years earlier when John
Browne wrote 'To what place are the thoughts
and desires of the great mass of visitors turned the
first thing every morning? To the Sands! To the
Sands! The merry, pleasant Sands. Such beautiful
sands as we have are not to be found at any other
watering place.'

Once the tide had gone out the firm wet sand,
found in abundance at Bridlington, was ideal for
walking, castle building, donkey riding, and the
location of a great range of stalls and entertainments. In 1900 the Corporation had a scale of

charges which allowed ice-cream or 'hokey pokey' stands, oyster barrows, photographic carts or tents, phonographic machines, tea or coffee stalls, musicians, vocalists, Punch and Judy shows, phrenologists and palmists on the sands. Coconut and 'Aunt Sally' stands were not allowed. Two stands, 20 feet square, were provided by the Corporation for troupes of pierrots or minstrels on the North Sands in 1901.

There were minstrel groups with blacked faces performing on the beach at Bridlington by the 1880s. In the late 1890s the two established minstrel groups, the Black Star Minstrels and the Waterloo Minstrels, amalgamated to form the resort's first resident pierrots, the Waterloo Pierrots. They had whitened faces and wore the distinctive white costume with ruffles and a conical hat.

There were donkeys on the sands by the early 1860s but they were not officially allowed onto the North Beach until 1896. Riders mounted the

The North Sands c. 1900. *(East Riding of Yorkshire Council)* It is packed with stalls. Pierrots are performing on a stage in the middle distance.

Mrs Bullock and Mrs Welbourne outside Holy Trinity Church, Bridlington. *(East Riding of Yorkshire Council)* They looked after the bathing machines that were 'parked' overnight in Trinity Cut. Were they also 'dippers', the women who helped you bathe?

A 'hokey pokey' man (ice-cream seller) on the North Sands c. 1895. *(Bayle Museum Trust)* From just before the First World War Rileys and Bakers were the main Bridlington ice-cream makers. Bakers did not close down until 1987.

donkeys, which were under the care of Mary Knaggs, at the top end of the Promenade adjoining Beaconsfield Gardens and reached the beach via Trinity Cut. By 1903 there were 47 licensed donkeys at work on Bridlington sands.

The sedate sea bathing of the Georgian period when visitors did little more than dip themselves into the sea with the help of an attendant gave way to more boisterous swimming from the 1850s. There were outcries against mixed bathing and beaches became segregated. The wearing of swimming costumes was by no means universal and in 1871 there was a call for the Bridlington Local Board to introduce a byelaw making it compulsory for bathers to wear 'drawers'. In 1879 'an observer' was shocked to see 'a young lady' bathing from a machine at Bridlington 'in a perfect state of nudity'.

Segregated swimming was a deterrent for families with young children and in 1900 Bridlington was a pioneer in introducing mixed bathing areas, with compulsory neck-to-knee costumes. Bathing tents hastened the demise of the bathing machine.

Bathing tents on the South Sands c. 1912. *(East Riding of Yorkshire Council)* The Spa Theatre and Opera House is in the distance.

Edwardian recreations

The chief attractions of Bridlington for the Edwardian gentleman visitor or the Hull merchant settling in Hilderthorpe were not the beach, promenades or concert halls but the opportunity to sail one's yacht or play a round of golf.

One of the finest sights at Bridlington is that of yachts in full sail racing across the Bay during the annual regatta of the Royal Yorkshire Yacht Club, held at the resort since 1904. The Royal Yorkshire Yacht Club (R.Y.Y.C) was formed by merchants and shipowners from Hull and Whitby in 1847 and in that year the club planned a regatta at Bridlington. There is no further mention of the R.Y.Y.C at the resort until 1871 when the club offered trophies for yacht races at the recently revived regatta. By 1898 three yacht clubs were sailing out of Bridlington harbour, the R.Y.Y.C, the Pirate Yacht Club and the Yorkshire Corinthian Yacht Club.

Bridlington Golf Club,
Hilderthorpe Hall.
(East Riding of Yorkshire Council)

Regatta, Bridlington Harbour c. 1900. *(East Riding of Yorkshire Council)* The yachts are moored at the South Pier. Note the recently built New Spa in the distance on the right, and the Norwegian villas on the left.

Golf was all the rage in Britain at the turn of the century and in June 1902 the first Bridlington golf course was laid out on land belonging to Flat Top Farm, Hilderthorpe. This course closed in 1909 by which time the present Bridlington Golf Club had been formed and an 18-hole course laid out on the Hilderthorpe Estate with the Hall converted to the clubhouse. The course was ready for play in May 1907.

The Borough of Bridlington

Under the Local Government Act of 1894 the Local Board was superseded by Bridlington Urban District Council, which had its first meeting on 9 January 1895. Soon afterwards one of the councillors, a solicitor, Walter Townsend, launched a campaign to have the town incorporated as a municipal borough. Queen Victoria was successfully petitioned and she signed a Charter of Incorporation on July 15 1899. Elections were held and when the council had its first meeting on 9 November 1899 the Borough of Bridlington came into being.

Robert Medforth, first Mayor of Bridlington, 1899. *(East Riding of Yorkshire Council)*

Bridlington Grammar School
c. 1905. (*Christopher Ketchell*)
Designed by John Bilson of
Hull, the school was extended
in 1901.

The Bridlington Corporation Act passed in
1904 gave the Council increased powers which
enabled it to take over the cemetery on Sewerby
Road, to establish electricity works in Brett Street
in 1905, to widen Cross Street in the same year
and St John Street by the First World War. Already
in 1903 the Corporation had become the Education Authority and in that year the last Board
School, the Oxford Street Schools (later Moor-
field Primary School) was opened. The first
school built by the Corporation was the Burlington School, Marton Road in 1910.

The re-founded Grammar School had been
opened on 9 August 1899, just before the Borough was established. Through the initiative of
Thomas Harland, solicitor and Lord Feoffee, a
scheme was devised whereby the funds of defunct
charities were used to endow the Grammar
School. Additional funds came from the sale of
charity land for housing and the gift of £1800
from the Lords Feoffees, the proceeds of their sale
to the Corporation in 1900 of the right to hold
markets and fairs. The Grammar School was an
immediate success under Arthur Thornton, head-
master 1899-1928. The Bridlington High School
for Girls, a joint venture of the Borough Council
and the County Council, was opened at the Elms,
St John Street in 1905. It also had a remarkable
long-serving head in Miss Edith Drummond,
1905-35. Both schools quickly established an envi-
able reputation.

The First World War

As well as causing the tragic loss of so many men World War I had a devastating effect on the economy of seaside resorts which had been experiencing a phenomenal growth in popularity. Britain entered the war on 4 August 1914 at the height of the holiday season, but the impact was not immediate. By the following summer the trade of Bridlington was seriously affected with apartment owners and shopkeepers recording a marked drop in income. The Corporation's revenue was also down with a substantial cut in the takings at the Prince's Parade and Spa and many rates not paid.

A reporter from the *Yorkshire Weekly Post* who visited Bridlington in early September 1915 found things going on as usual with the Prince's Parade showing 'no signs of having suffered from the effects of the war. The flower beds are as bloomingly gay as ever. The floral clock seems as floral as before, and the hall has its baskets as beautiful as at any other time. Both the band here and on the New Spa are conducted as usual by Signor Scoma and Mr Julian Kandt respectively'. But the place had a strangely deserted appearance, where it was usual to see thousands, there were only hundreds. 'You may write to half-a-dozen boarding houses, and find that any one of them can spare you a room, or rooms, for your family if you

New recruits outside the recruiting office at the corner of West Street on South Cliff Road, 1914. *(East Riding of Yorkshire Council)* How many of these came back? Three hundred and twenty men from Bridlington were killed in the war.

War damage, Bridlington, 1918. *(East Riding of Yorkshire Council)* On 1 May 1918 a German mine exploded close to the Beaconsfield Sea Wall. No lives were lost but many houses were damaged as far away as Marshall Avenue. The buildings fronting the sea and those nearby on Promenade lost most of their windows and ceilings, doors and roofs were damaged.

O. H. M. S.

NOTICE.

ORDER by Brigadier General N. T. Nickalls, Commanding York-shire Mounted Brigade, made and published pursuant to the Defence of the Realm (Consolidation) Regulations 1914.

It is hereby required that within the area East of an imaginary line drawn due north and south from the **CRAB ROCKS** to the **Seashore** at **SEWERBY** village between the hours of 4-30 p.m. and 7-30 a.m. **all Persons** shall remain within doors, except such persons as shall be in possession of a permit in writing signed by me or some person duly authorised by me.

APPLICATIONS FOR PERMITS under this order should be made personally to the OFFICER COMMANDING QUEEN'S OWN YORK-SHIRE DRAGOONS YEOMANRY RESERVE, ALEXANDRA HOTEL, BRIDLINGTON.

N. T. NICKALLS,

BRIGADIER GENERAL.
Hornsea. Commanding Yorkshire Mounted Brigade.

GREEN & SON, PRINTERS, MARKET PLACE, BEVERLEY.

Notice ordering a night-time curfew on Flamborough headland during World War I. *(Bayle Musem Trust)*

wish it.' There was no sign of the tripper and the fortnightly visitors had not turned up in their usual numbers. There was no pleasure steamer but boatmen were still plying for hire, dismissing the threat of mines and submarines. The reporter saw seven minesweepers at the mouth of the harbour.

Hotels and boarding houses were requisitioned for military use, troops were billeted in the town and parts of the beach to the north and south were closed and used for training exercises. The soldiers dug trenches and prepared for the fields of France. On 22 November 1914 the head of Burlington Council School noted in the log book: 'The gardeners of Class X were marched to the north shore at 9.30 a.m. and returned at 12.30 p.m. One squad continued the deepening of the military trenches started by the Civil Guard on Saturday and Sunday whilst the other under the direction of a lieutenant of the Yorks dragoons measured out and started digging new trenches'. Later entries record German airships passing over Bridlington late at night on their way to bomb Hull on 2 -3 March 1916 (they used Flamborough lighthouse as a guide) and the sending of 24 scarves, 24 pairs of socks and 12 pairs of mittens knitted by the girls in a fortnight to the War Department.

Peace

The entry made by the headteacher in the log book for 16-18 July 1919 notes that the school was closed for 'Peace Celebrations'. Bridlington celebrated the coming of peace in a memorable way

with an 'Historic Review', better known as the Peace Pageant, masterminded by Robert Horspool, art master at Bridlington Grammar School. On Wednesday and Thursday 16-17 July hundreds of townspeople, young and old, processed around the town dressed in costumes depicting people and events from the history of Bridlington, ranging from ancient Britons to 'Paul Jones and his Crew of Pirates'. The procession started at the recreation ground and ended at the High Green.

At the High Green an 'Old World Fair' was recreated with archery, skittles, bowls, quarterstaff and other traditional games. The fair was followed by dancing on the green, to the prizewinning Excelsior Band conducted by Henry Harper.

The Peace Pageant has had one lasting legacy, the Bridlington Augustinian Society. Those involved in research for the pageant decided that the enthusiasm for the study of the history of the town that it had engendered should not be lost. A year later, on 15 July 1920, they formed an antiquarian society called the Augustinians 'for the purpose of collecting, recording and preserving relics of Bridlington and district'. It was decided to use the titles of the Augustinian canons for the officers, with the secretary known as the Scribe, and the chairman known as the Prior. The society still flourishes.

Peace Pageant on Promenade, July 1919. *(Bayle Museum Trust)* The ancient Britons are just passing Grays, boot and shoe dealer (21 Promenade) and the Druids are passing Garlands, bookshop and stationer (23 Promenade).

Poster publicising the Peace Pageant 1919. *(Bayle Museum Trust)*

The founders of Bridlington
Augustinian Society, 1920.
(Bayle Museum Trust). They are
from left to right R. Horspool,
M. Lawson, S. Charlesworth,
E. Taylor and F.W. Lendis.
Sydney Charlesworth was
the first Prior of the Society.
An engineer, he was a town
councillor, Harbour Commissioner,
and Assistant Lord Feoffee;
Robert Horspool, art master
at the Grammar School, was a
Lord Feoffee; Major Lawson
had a shoe shop on Chapel
Street and was a Lord Feofeee;
Fred Lendis was the manager
of the Bridlington Free Press
and a town councillor; and
Edgar Taylor was the
proprietor of Rowntree and
Taylor's Café, Promenade.

Civic Pride

The First World War might have interrupted Bridlington's progress but once peace had arrived the Corporation took great pains to promote the resort. They were particularly concerned with increasing the town's amenities. In 1919, after having leased it for five years, they bought the Spa and six years later knocked down the last of the 1890s buildings. On the site they built the Spa Royal Hall at a cost of £50,000. Opened 15 July 1926 this spacious Art Deco building was the envy of the other East Coast Resorts. When the hall was destroyed by fire, on the night of 29 January 1932, it was replaced by the present Spa Royal Hall, built in 52 days to the designs of Peter Newton, the able borough architect.

After much discussion about its future the Corporation had the old Grand Pavilion at the north end of the Prince's Parade demolished in November 1936. This opened up the sea front and, following a public outcry, previous plans to rebuild on the site were scrapped. Instead a new ultra-modern style Grand Pavilion, designed by Peter Newton, was built on Victoria Terrace Gardens, fronting on Promenade. This building, opened 12 July 1937, is now incorporated in Leisure World.

Newton was also the architect of the Corporation's flagship building, the former Town Hall on the site of the White Lodge, Quay Road. Opened on 11 May 1932 this handsome fifteen-bay building in a late Wren style has an entrance hall with a grand marble staircase leading to the council chamber and a large ballroom.

Bridlington Town Hall 1932. *(Bayle Museum Trust)*

Entrance to the Spa Royal Hall, 1926. *(East Riding of Yorkshire Council)* The hall was designed by Blackmore, Sykes & Co. of Hull.

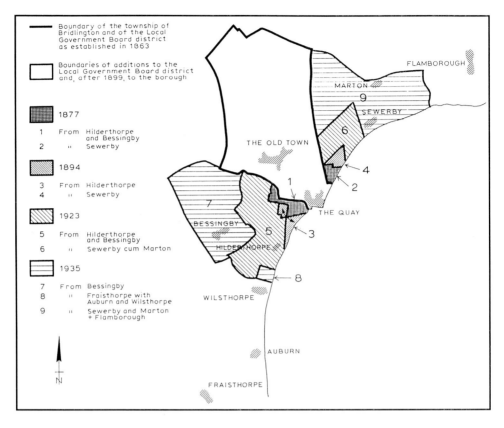

The following is the legend content within the map figure:

Boundary of the township of
Bridlington and of the Local
Government Board district
as established in 1863

Boundaries of additions to the
Local Government Board district
and, after 1899, to the borough

1877

1   From   Hilderthorpe
            and Bessingby
2   "   Sewerby

1894

3   From   Hilderthorpe
4   "   Sewerby

1923

5   From   Hilderthorpe
            and Bessingby
6   "   Sewerby cum Marton

1935

7   From   Bessingby
8   "   Fraisthorpe with
            Auburn and Wilsthorpe
9   "   Sewerby and Marton
            + Flamborough

N

FLAMBOROUGH
MARTON
9
SEWERBY
6
THE OLD TOWN
1
7
4
2
THE QUAY
BESSINGBY
5
3
HILDERTHORPE
8
WILSTHORPE
AUBURN
FRAISTHORPE

Bridlington Boundary Extensions (plan by Keith Scurr reproduced by permission from S. Neave and S. Ellis (eds), *An Historical Atlas of East Yorkshire*, The University of Hull Press, 1996)

Another of the achievements of the inter-war Council was the establishment of a public library. In this Bridlington had lagged behind many other towns. The library began in October 1926 in a small building on Quay Road. Initially it only opened two evenings a week and had a small stock of non-fiction books and six novels. Ten years later the former Midland Bank (14 King Street) was purchased by the Council and after alteration was opened as the new public library on 28 June 1937.

The Borough Council, acting with the East Riding County Council, built two schools at this period; St George's Senior Boys School opened 10 September 1935 and St George's Senior Girls School opened 5 May 1938. In 1944 they became St George's County Secondary Schools, then in 1965 the Headlands Lower School. Part is now East Yorkshire College.

Bridlington Corporation took three bold steps to preserve the environment of the area by purchasing Sewerby House and Park in 1934, the Danes Dyke Estate in 1935 and finally

Grand Pavilion 1937. *(R. Hartley)*

Sewerby Park. Advertisement from *Bridlington Guide*, 1939. *(East Riding of Yorkshire Council)*

Flamborough Head in 1939 to prevent it being overrun with bungalows. Danes Dyke and Flamborough Head had long been the haunt of the Bridlington holidaymaker but Sewerby Park had been the private property of the Lloyd-Greame family. The Corporation rapidly developed the hall and park for visitors. The grounds were laid out for golf, bowls and archery, the stables became a milk bar, the eighteenth-century hall was converted to a café and restaurant and in the grounds a ladies orchestra played in the newly-built bandstand. Sewerby House (later renamed Sewerby Hall) and Park were officially opened by Amy Johnson on 1 June 1936.

Between the Wars

Bridlington soon recovered after the war and, if newspaper reports are to be believed, it was even more popular than before. With longer holidays and, for some, higher wages and holidays with pay, more people could get to the seaside. Some indication of the popularity of Bridlington can be gleaned from the 1921 census which, because of industrial disputes, had to be put back from April to June. The population of the borough on 19 June was 23,101, a staggering rise from 14,334 in 1911, but this included 7,558 visitors. In terms of seaside visitor numbers Bridlington was 8th in the country in a list headed by Blackpool. It was not far below Scarborough with 8,682 visitors and Brighton with 7,691.

In 1931 the population of Bridlington was 19,705 showing a substantial rise in the number of residents since 1921. Much of the rise in population came from the development of the estates

Wooden bungalow and car
at Wilsthorpe, early 1930s.
(R. Hartley)

each side of Forty Foot Road and local authority housing.

On August Bank Holiday 1935 the *Bridlington Chronicle* calculated that the number of visitors was 50,000 and that the population of the town that day was 80,000. Not only did the numbers of visitors increase but their mode of travel, length of stay and choice of accommodation changed. In May 1921 the local newspapers were reporting a decrease in the rail services and an increase in motor traffic, and in July that year a daily 'char-a-banc' service began from Leeds to Bridlington for the season. Each year the increase in road traffic was noted. To provide for this the Corporation carried out road improvements including co-operating with the County Council in the building of Kingsgate which was officially opened on 31 July 1923. The trains were not abandoned and on the August Bank Holiday weekend in 1935 75,619 people arrived at the station.

Visitors were not staying so long. In 1918 it was thought that 'the holiday maker who stayed for a month or six weeks had gone for ever' and many new visitors were choosing camp sites for cheaper holidays free from the 'irksome rules' of boarding houses. Although many stayed in tents, others rented converted railway carriages or buses, ex-army huts or wooden bungalows. In June 1932 there were said to be 'scores of tents' on the north side extending right along to Danes Dyke, and the camping ground near Charity Farm, Sewerby, was tightly packed. On the south side were the recently-established Corporation camping site at South Cliff and the popular site on Grainger's Farm at Wilsthorpe. The camps were not popular with local residents. In July 1939 a boarding house keeper claimed that 'there are enough people at Wilsthorpe to fill all the houses, and here we are with no one'.

In great contrast to the camps was the Expanse Hotel erected on the North Shore in 1937 by a Horsforth builder E. C. Briggs. Modern in style and facilities it had 38 bedrooms, all of which had a bathroom adjacent and ten were en-suite. The spacious dining room doubled as a ballroom, an orchestra was engaged and 'the latest type of instrument for reproducing music' had been installed.

Inter-war entertainments

Between the wars the most popular venues were the Spa Royal Hall and the Floral Pavilion. The main attraction at the latter was the fine concert orchestra under directors such as Garadini (1923-26; 1929) and Lionel Johns (1933-40) but at the Spa Royal Hall it was Herman Darewski, the man who got Bridlington dancing.

Darewski was musical director at the Spa for ten seasons in the years 1924-39. He recalled in his autobiography that when he first went to the Spa, 'concerts finished at 9.30 every evening, which seemed an absurd hour for the people to be sent home with no other form of entertainment available — I realised that dancing would become a craze ... It is no exaggeration to say the intro-duction of the Darewski Dances as they were called, created a furore'.

A host of new entertainment venues opened in the 1920s-30s all located on Promenade. The wooden Floral Hall, between Albion Terrace and Carlisle Road, was opened in May 1921 by the proprietors of the Alexandra Hotel. It was burnt down in August 1923, the night before George Robey was to appear. Public tennis courts took its place.

The most impressive façade on Promenade was that of the Winter Gardens. Opened as the Coli-seum in 1922 it was renamed in 1924. It had a theatre with seating for 1,300 and a ballroom in the basement. The ballroom later became a roller rink and then a billiards saloon, and the theatre a cinema. The cinema closed in 1982 and the build-ing has since been demolished. The Lounge on the opposite side of Promenade and stretching back to Esplanade, formerly Fields Café, was

The Expanse Hotel c. 1938. The two top floors had sun balconies and below were underground garages. It was altered in 1954-5 and lost some of its rounded edges.

The Great Darewski 1936. (*Bayle Museum Trust*) Darewski was a composer of well-known songs including 'Sister Susie's Sewing Shirts for Soldiers', 'K-K-K-Katy', 'Ours is a Nice 'Ouse, Ours is' and 'Where Do Flies Go in the Winter Time?'. Over 3,500 attended the first evening concert of Darewski's last season at Bridlington in 1939.

Covers from official publicity leaflets and guides:
(facing page) 1927 guide with old Grand Pavilion in background;
(this page top) 1938 leaflet with Spa Theatre and Spa Royal Hall in background;
(this page bottom) 1939 leaflet with new Grand Pavilion in centre.
(East Riding of Yorkshire Council).

The new entertainment. Fun City Amusement Arcade, North Marine Drive. *(East Riding of Yorkshire Council)* Built in 1923 it was one of seven amusement arcades at the resort by 1939. In May 1937 Councillor Albert Wilkinson, speaking at the annual meeting of the Lords Feoffees and Assistants of the Manor, described 'pin tables' as 'the curse of Bridlington'.

opened as 'one of finest cafés and concert rooms on the coast' in June 1927. It was gutted by fire five months later, but re-opened the next year as the Esplanade Café and Lounge Theatre. The theatre was showing 'talkies' in 1931.

The sands

With the expansion of the town to the north and south and the extending of the sea defences and building of promenades, a greater area of the seafront came into regular use. South of the harbour the Corporation extended the Spa Wall and laid out the Princess Mary Promenade in 1925-8. To the north the wooden Sewerby Sea Defences were rebuilt in stone in 1929-31 and the North Marine Drive laid out behind.

The activities on the sands changed little. There were fewer stalls and entertainers, pierrots gave way to concert parties but there were still Punch and Judy shows, donkeys and the ice-cream sellers. Bathing machines finally went, and bathing tents and deckchairs, which could be hired, appeared in greater numbers. By 1930 bathing bungalows, adjoining the Spa and on the Belvedere Sea Wall, could be hired for 15s (75p) a week in the season.

Sandcastle building was encouraged through sponsored competitions. Children, families and

A donkey ride on the south sands in the 1920s. *(East Riding of Yorkshire Council)*

even boarding houses competed against each other producing magnificent structures that were soon destroyed by the incoming tide. Also in the 1920s-30s could be seen the work of the one-armed sand artist, John 'Lawty' Jenkinson from Filey. On the smooth sands he drew pictures of horses, cathedrals, local churches and fantastic designs.

A holidaymaker remembers how '"Snaps" photographers roamed the beach as well as the pier and the Esplanade, 'shooting' everyone in sight. They gave you a ticket, which you took to their shop near the pier, to view the photographs and buy them if you liked them.' Foster Brigham founded 'Snaps' in 1920 and he secured the sole rights of photography on Bridlington beach. He was soon employing an army of uniformed photographers.

The harbour

'From early morning until the late hour at night the North Pier was the hub of the town.'

Bridlington Chronicle,
August Bank Holiday 1935.

The Burton family on the north sands, 1924. A 'Snaps' photograph. *(C..M. Burton)*

For many a trip in a boat was the great attraction. The visitor could go out in a coble fishing with rod and line, have the thrill of a speedboat ride or enjoy a trip in a steamer to 'Flamber'ed'. Between the wars the main pleasure boats were the *Frenchman*, a paddle steamer, in use from 1899 to 1928, the steam tug *Yorkshireman* from 1928, the *Princess Marina*, the *Boys Own*, the *Royal Sovereign* and the *Yorkshire Belle*.

Watching the fishing boats was another pastime. The fishing industry was the mainstay of the

The pleasure steamer *Yorkshireman* entering Bridlington Harbour c. 1950. *(East Riding of Yorkshire Council)*

Newly-caught fish lined up on the South Pier, January 1935. *(East Riding of Yorkshire Council)*

port although it had many problems in the 1920s-30s. There were 53 motor cobles fishing out of Bridlington in 1920 but this had dropped to 28 motor cobles and fourteen sailing cobles by 1928. At this date 144 men were employed in the industry. The lack of fish and the increased cost of transporting it led some fishermen to rely chiefly on the tourist trade.

Annual events to be seen from the North Pier included the regatta, the sea angling festival, which began in 1922, and the 'aquatic' sports held as part of the town carnival. Alongside the harbour in Queen's Square there were swimming baths kept by 'Professor' Gautier in the 1920s-30s. Gautier, self-styled 'Houdini of the Water' gave exhibitions each day, diving off the North Pier at high tide.

T.E. Lawrence, 'Lawrence of Arabia', as Aircraftsman Shaw knew the harbour well in the 1930s. He was at Bridlington at least three times, the longest period during the winter of 1934-5 when he was overseeing the refitting of ten R.A.F. armoured target boats stationed in the harbour.

The Second World War

The day war broke out, 3 September 1939, was the day the T.U.C. began its annual conference at Bridlington. The hotels, including the newly-opened Expanse, and boarding houses were going to be full, but the number of delegates was reduced by a quarter because of the 'international situation'.

The impact of the Second World War on the resort was far more sudden and severe than that of the First World War. In 1940 the *Bridlington Chronicle* reported that August Bank Holiday Monday was 'hardly any different from any other day of the last few months. There were no more than the usual number of people, practically all residents, taking a walk or shopping in the town. The portions of the beach which have been left open for bathing ... were crowded, but otherwise there was nothing to signify that it was August Bank Holiday in Bridlington.' The lack of visitors is hardly surprising because over the previous month numerous bombs had been dropped on the resort by German aircraft and several people killed. The Civil Defence incidents book for Bridlington records many occasions when bombs fell on the town between June 1940 and March 1945. The last, in Kingsgate, was an isolated incident, the first recorded since October 1941.

Understandably the harbour was a prime target and the area of the town to the north and west was the most severely affected. On Thursday 11 July 1940 two bombs fell on Prince Street and Hilderthorpe Road, and two men and three women were killed. Twice in August Prince Street was hit again destroying the Britannia Hotel, the Cock and Lion as well as Foley's Café and part of Woolworths. The pleasure boat *Royal Britannia* was destroyed in the harbour. One woman and a soldier were killed and eleven people had to be dug out of a cellar. The buildings destroyed or severely damaged in 1940-41 included the Post Office, the Corporation's new electricity showrooms and St Anne's Convalescent Home. The station goods yard was also hit.

Many evacuees, mainly mothers and children, were sent to Bridlington during the war as it was classed as a Reception area. For a time boys from Riley High School, Hull took over part of the Grammar School buildings and girls from

Tom Alderson, the A.R.P leader, who was awarded the first George Cross for his work rescuing 21 people following the 1940 raids. *(Bayle Museum Trust)*

FOOD is a MUNITION OF WAR

Learn to make the most of your food by attending a series of

WAR-TIME COOKERY DEMONSTRATIONS

to be held in the

Gas Showrooms, Quay Road

from MONDAY, April 27th, to FRIDAY, May 1st, inclusive, at 3-0 p.m. daily

DEMONSTRATOR FROM THE MINISTRY OF FOOD ADVICE CENTRE

ADMISSION FREE   EVERYONE INVITED

Notice from *Bridlington Free Press* 25 April 1942

The Britannia

The ruins of the Britannia Hotel after the raid on 21 August 1940. *(Bayle Museum Trust)*

Newland High School, Hull were accommodated at the High School.

The threat of an invasion and the number of air-raid warnings led thousands of residents to move away, most temporarily, and at times there were hundreds of empty homes. Alderman Tom Fenby, the blacksmith from St John Street who had been M.P. for East Bradford was mayor 1939-44. In a speech at York in August 1940 he highlighted the plight of Bridlington which 'was sorely stricken and what boarding house keepers were going to do in the winter they did not know'.

Throughout the war Bridlington was subjected to a total blackout at night and for part of the war there was a curfew lasting from 10 p.m. to 6 a.m. Thousands of military personnel and their equipment, including tanks were based in the town. Soldiers were billeted in hotels and boarding houses and at the Spa. Their numbers were swelled by those coming to the town in the evening from nearby R.A.F. bases.

Rebuilding

With the ending of the war in May 1945 came the rebuilding. One of the first actions taken by the Corporation was the development of an industrial estate south of Bessingby Road, in a move to bring light industry to the town to relieve the ever-present problem of winter unemployment. In 1948 the Corporation proposed to centre future industrial development at Carnaby.

With 1,277 families in the town 'inadequately housed' new housing was a priority. Temporary 'prefabs' were erected and plans were made for a new Corporation estate off Bessingby Road. Eighty-six acres of land were compulsorily purchased and the first house on the West Hill estate ready by August 1949. The award winning estate, designed by Clifford E. Culpin of London, was of a very high standard.

A radical plan drawn up for Bridlington by the East Riding planning office in 1948, to deal with increased traffic at the Quay, was fortunately sh lved and a one-way system for Chapel Street, Cross Street, Queen Street and Manor Street introduced in 1950. Blitzed buildings were slowly rebuilt. Work on a new Post Office began in November 1949 but the St Anne's Convalescent Home was not rebuilt, as St Anne's Homes, until 1959-60.

Post-war resort

As soon as the war was over it was business as usual at the resort, although the Expanse Hotel and the Alexandra Hotel did not re-open until May 1948 and April 1949 respectively. They had been occupied by the forces during the war.

The brochure produced for the 1946 season had all the familiar ingredients. Raymond de Courcy and his orchestra were booked for two concerts daily in the Floral Pavilion and Ceres Harper and his New Dance Orchestra were appearing for the season at the Spa Royal Hall. A 'super summer revue Gaiety Fayre, with an all-star cast including Freddie Foss', was at the Grand Pavilion and the Harry Hanson Court Players were performing the latest and best West End plays at the Spa Theatre. (In 1950 Brian Rix and the Viking Theatre Company were at the Spa Theatre.)

Francis Johnson (1911-95), architect, magistrate, councillor and Lord Feoffee.*(Bayle Museum Trust)* This picture shows him as a councillor in 1936. Dr Francis Johnson was Chief Lord five times. He designed the St Anne's Homes and many other buildings in Bridlington and East Yorkshire. He fought long and hard to preserve the character of the Old Town.

Bridlington Prices 1947	
Fish and chips (to take out)	9d (4p) and 1s (5p)
High tea with roast duck etc	4/6 (22½p)
Ice cream	3d (1p)
Donkey rides	6d (2½p)
Deck chairs	6d (2½p)
Dancing	2s (10p) to 3/6 (17½p)

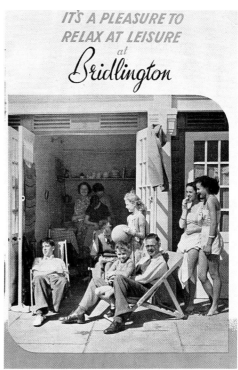

The 1950s have been described as 'the last golden decade of domestic seaside resorts' (J. Demetriadi). It was a time of full employment and of holidays with pay. The mass of the population holidayed in Britain. The seaside visitor was generally content with the level of accommodation and the entertainment provided. Television had not yet made inroads into the popularity of the revues and other live shows. (In 1950 there were only 14 television licences in the Bridlington postal area; by September 1953, thanks to the Coronation, this had risen to 1,811.) Despite the dramatic increase in car ownership many still travelled by rail and were more likely to choose a holiday destination with which they were familiar.

There were 40 private hotels and 206 boarding houses and apartments seeking customers in the 1946 brochure, but such traditional accommodation was under threat. The popularity of camp sites evident before the war continued but tents, converted railway carriages and wooden shacks soon gave way to caravans. By 1953 the six

Post-war guides to the town: *(facing page)* 1949 guide; *(above left)* mid-1950s leaflet; *(above right)* bathing bungalow brochure c. 1957.

camping sites in the Borough of Bridlington were chiefly used for caravans in addition to the Corporation caravan site at South Cliff. Some 4,000 holidaymakers occupied the sites at the height of the summer season. Another innovation of the 1950s was the self-catering holiday flat. In the Bridlington guide for 1955 there was an advertisement for 'Furnished Holiday Flatlets — The New Idea' and the following year one for 'Go as you please holidays — why not a Flatlet'. By 1973 the guide had over 175 advertisements for holiday flats.

Mr Palmer's Punch and Judy on the North Sands 1952. (Eric Palmer) One of the traditional ingredients of the seaside.

There can be no doubt that 1950-60 was Bridlington's last golden decade. The pre-war prosperity seemed to be returning, visitor numbers were on the increase and the resident population was rising. In 1951 Bridlington ranked 30th in terms of population out of 116 English and Welsh seaside resorts.

From the early 1960s difficulties began for the resort. Rail travel declined and in 1965 Bridlington lost its direct line to West and South Yorkshire, the traditional source of many of its visitors. Car ownership encouraged many to explore new, less accessible destinations and holidays abroad became more commonplace for the middle classes. The annual holiday was no longer automatically a week or fortnight at the same seaside resort year after year. There was a growth in the proportion of 'low-spend' visitors and day trippers, and a consequent decline in facilities and a failure to update and maintain accommodation.

'Neglected', Bridlington, 1965. (M. Holland)

Three of the four cinemas closed; the Lounge in 1961, the Roxy in 1962 and the Regal (ABC) in 1971, and two large hotels were demolished; the Victoria on Promenade in 1974 and the vast Alexandra in 1975. The loss of the Alexandra was particularly significant as its opening in 1866 had demonstrated confidence in a future for the Victorian resort. Other losses included the town's top department stores, Carltons and Allens, which were closed in 1968 and 1977 respectively. Both were subsequently demolished.

There were however several positive developments taking place. In 1970 Hammonds, later Binns, department store (now occupied by Boyes) was opened on the site of Carltons. After stagnating in the 1960s the population steadily rose from the 1970s and there was much new housing. The

Corporation invested in education and the cultural life of the town opening a new secondary school, Headlands School, in September 1965 and extending the public library in 1966 and again in 1973. Bridlington also got a swimming pool in 1973, an amenity that had been called for 50 years before.

The boom in the fishing industry after the Second World War continued with a change from line-fishing to the more lucrative inshore trawling. Thanks to outside investment the numbers of boats operating out of Bridlington steadily increased, particularly after the opening of the new fish quay buildings on the South Pier in 1975. In 1987 Bridlington was ranked the seventh largest fishing port in England and Wales.

Population of Bridlington	
1931	19,705
1951	24,661
1961	26,023
1971	26,776
1981	29,219
1991	32,158

The decline that Bridlington experienced from the early 1960s was common to all British seaside resorts but there were additional factors. The slump in northern industries from the 1970s had a disastrous effect on the number of week- or fortnight-long visitors to Bridlington. Those coming for the traditional 'Scottish fortnight' dramatically decreased with the collapse of heavy engineering in Scotland and the number of longer stay visitors from West and South Yorkshire declined with the reduction in textile manufacture, the rationalisation of the steel industry and pit closures. A survey of visitors in August and September 1986 revealed that over half those interviewed were day visitors with nearly 75 per cent of all visitors coming from Yorkshire and eleven per cent from the East Midlands.

There were plenty of schemes for reviving the resort, including the building of a marina for which there were abortive plans in 1969, 1973 and 1988. A proposal for a 'Paradise Island' leisure project on Limekiln Lane in 1981 was headlined in the *Bridlington Free Press*: 'Paradise — or the way down? Complex answer to town's desperate problem'. The opening of more and larger amusement arcades exacerbated the problem rather than providing a solution with the low point coming in the mid-1980s when the Prince's Parade was turned over to a fun fair. The 'floral clock' was removed to Sewerby Park in 1985 and in September 1986 the final concert was held in the Floral Pavilion, part of which soon afterwards housed a ghost train.

Bridlington Harbour, 1964 by Walter Goodin. *(East Riding of Yorkshire Council)* Walter Goodin (1907-92), a former railway porter, was trained by the artist Fred Elwell. He spent his later life at Bridlington and produced many fine views of the town and neighbourhood.

Regeneration

Just as the future looked particularly bleak the town was given a great boost by winning the 'Resorts 2000' competition held by the English Tourist Board. The tourist board had launched the nation-wide competition in 1985 in an attempt to stimulate strategies to revive the English seaside. The successful Bridlington strategy devised by the local authorities (Borough of East Yorkshire and Humberside County Council) with the support of local organisations received development aid from the tourist board. One result was the Bridlington Improvement Project involving the Lords Feoffees, the Civic Society, the Harbour Commissioners, the Bridlington Self-Catering Association, Bridlington Free Press, Bridlington School, the Chamber of Trade, the Hotel and Guest House Association and the East Yorkshire Borough Council. The project initiated many schemes for improving the environment of the Old Town and Quay.

Improvements in the facilities of the town and the resort since the mid-1980s have included Leisure World, opened 1987, the new Bridlington Hospital, opened 1989, and the increased investment in Sewerby Hall and Park, now housing the museum of the East Riding and hosting a range of cultural events.

As a result of local government re-organisation Bridlington lost its borough status on 1 April 1974 and it was taken into the larger Borough of North Wolds (later renamed East Yorkshire) within the administrative County of Humberside. Following a further re-organisation on 1 April 1996 Bridlington became part of the area of the East Riding of Yorkshire Council, a unitary authority with headquarters at Beverley. From April 2000 Bridlington will, in addition, have its own parish (town) council, albeit with limited powers.

The refurbished Spa and Princess Mary Promenades *(East Riding of Yorkshire Council)*

Beside the Seaside Museum, Queen Street opened May 1998. A major contribution by the Lords Feoffees to the regeneration of Bridlington. This interactive museum, designed by Mike Oakenfull and Francis Johnson and Partners, tells the story of Bridlington as a resort.

The new Emmanuel Church, Cardigan Road, built 1998. Designed by the leading Edinburgh firm of architects Law and Dunbar-Nasmith it replaced the early 20th-century building that was gutted by fire in August 1995.

Since the mid-1990s there has been an increasing air of optimism about the resort's future. More than anything else this has been due to the success of the rebuilding and refurbishment of the north and south promenades which has enabled a renewed appreciation of Bridlington's greatest assets, the sea, the beach and the harbour. But if longer-stay visitors with higher spending power are to be attracted back there needs to be improved accommodation, a greater range of shops, better leisure and cultural facilities, and a more attractive built environment. It is these issues, along with increased job opportunities and improved housing for the resident population, that are being successfully addressed by the Bridlington Regeneration Partnership, a consortium of nearly 40 local organisations together with the East Riding of Yorkshire Council, with its 'Building a Better Bridlington' programme launched in 1997. The Partnership along with the Harbour Commissioners, the Royal Yorkshire Yacht Club and the East Riding of Yorkshire Council is closely involved in the major project to build a marina to the south of the harbour, a scheme arousing much discussion at the beginning of the new Millennium.

STREETS AND BUILDINGS

The Old Town

Generally known as the 'Old Town' since the later 19th century, this area, the site of the original settlement of Bridlington, remains undiscovered by the hundreds of thousands of visitors who flock to the resort each year. Yet with its two medieval buildings, the Priory and the Bayle, fine merchants' houses and the unrivalled display of Georgian bow windows it should rank high in any list of tourist destinations in Yorkshire.

Although it is known from Domesday Book that there was a settlement before the founding of the priory in the early 12th century nothing is known about its location and topography. There

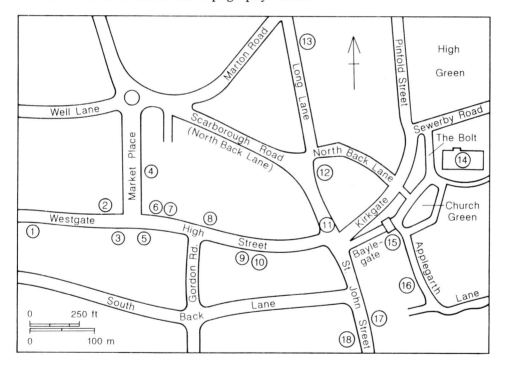

The Old Town *(plan by Mike Frankland)*

(1) The Avenue
(2) Site of Green Dragon Inn
(3) Hebblethwaite House, 7-9 Westgate
(4) Site of Corn Exchange
(5) Black Lion Inn
(6) Site of the medieval guildhall of St Mary
(7) Site of the Hustler mansion (Globe Inn)
(8) Manor House, 64 High Street
(9) William Kent's home, 45 High Street

(10) The Toft, 43 High Street
(11) Site of Black Bull Inn (George Inn)
(12) Former National School
(13) Site of the Union Workhouse
(14) The Priory Church
(15) The Bayle and site of Baptist chapel
(16) Baptist burial ground
(17) Site of first Methodist chapel
(18) Site of Zion Independent chapel

View north across Old Town from the tower of the electricity works, Brett Street, in 1905. *(F.F.Johnson)* St John Street is at the right of the picture. In the foreground is The Elms which was soon to become the Girls High School. It was the home of Dr Brett after whom the adjoining street was named

has been little archaeological investigation. The Priory church is almost certainly on the site of the Saxon church and it can be assumed that the early settlement clustered around it.

After the founding of the priory the town developed along the curving line of the present Kirkgate and High Street with a road running south towards the harbour, St John Street. Until the early 20th century this was narrow like the present High Street. The other main streets of the Old Town, the Market Place and Westgate, are wider, and in the case of the former more regular, suggesting a later planned development.

The Priory precinct

The area around the Priory church has undergone more change in the 20th century than any other part of the Old Town. All the older houses of the once narrow streets of Baylegate, Nungate (now Sewerby Road) and The Bolt have been swept away, as well as those on the north side of Church Green and the south side of Kirkgate. Much of the demolition took place just before and just after the First World War.

The ancient open spaces of High Green, which had a large circular pond filled in 1900-1, and Church or Low Green were the locations for annual fairs. The pleasure fair was held on High Green from 1879 until 1973. A number of the

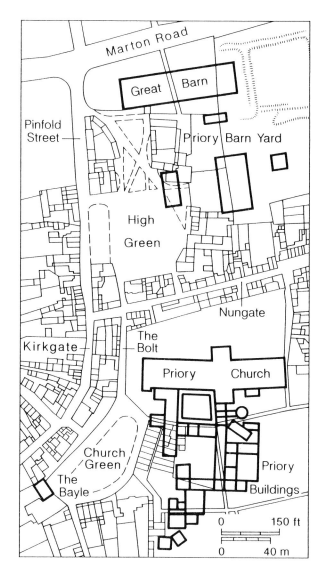

The conjectural layout of the Priory buildings on a street plan c. 1910. *(Drawing by Mike Frankland from plan by John Earnshaw)* Much of the area shown would have been within the precincts of the priory. There is no evidence of a wall enclosing the area although the priory was given permission to crenellate its buildings in 1388. The medieval gateway called the Bayle is of this date. The suffix 'gate' in the street names does not refer to a gateway but comes from the Scandinavian word 'gata' meaning street.

older buildings around High Green and along Pinfold Street incorporate priory stone.

On the north side of Church Green, just east of the Bayle, stood the Knitting School founded by William Bower in 1670 and the old Bull and Sun Inn. The latter was relocated to its present premises, a former draper's shop, in Baylegate c. 1920. Nearer the Priory church stood the George and Dragon Inn, demolished 1866. Its site was used as the playground for the adjoining National Infants' School, built 1857. The school closed in 1910 and was demolished soon after.

On the south side of Church Green were the 18th-century workhouse and a large Georgian

Looking east along Kirkgate c. 1900. *(East Riding of Yorkshire Council)* Much of the character of the area was lost when the buildings on the south side were cleared away. The older buildings that survive on the north side include 15-17 Kirkgate, late 17th or early 18th century, brick with stone plinth and rusticated quoins.

house, Priory Close, now rebuilt as the Priory Church Rooms. The present terraces are of the early and mid-19th century. Applegarth Lane, running south from Church Green, must take its name from the Priory orchard.

High Street

Until the later 17th century the present High Street, between St John Street and the Market Place, was part of a much longer Westgate. Although the name High Street was being used in the 1670s it was not in common usage until after 1710 and even then properties along the present High Street were often referred to as being in Westgate.

The High Street with its continuation Westgate was the principal street of Georgian Bridlington with the fine residences of merchants, apothecaries and attorneys intermingled with the shops and workshops of a great range of craftsmen and tradesmen. There were numerous inns, the chief of which was the George Inn (later the Black Bull), at the east end of High Street on the north side. It could boast a bowling green and a cockpit where vicious three-day cockfights were held in the mid-18th century. The National School was built at the end of its yard in 1826. Long closed, the inn or a successor building was swept away when Waterworks Street (later widened to become Scarborough Road) was laid out in the 1890s.

There were 100 properties in the High Street when they were first numbered around 1860. At this date 1 High Street was on the north side at the corner of Market Place, and the buildings

No. 70 High Street in the 1940s. *(Georgian Society for East Yorkshire)* It was the Trophy of Music inn in 1807, renamed the Bull and Butcher by 1819. It then became an ironmonger's shop, first Cranswicks then Milners.

were numbered consecutively ending on the south side with 100, the Black Lion Hotel. The street was renumbered c. 1902-5 from the east end with even numbers on the north side and odd numbers on the south side.

By the 1870s the rise of Bridlington Quay was challenging the Old Town's primacy as the commercial centre of the town. Yet on the eve of the First World War the High Street was still crammed with shops and workshops. In 1911 the street had seven grocers, four fruiterers (one also a fish dealer), five butchers, a tripe dealer, two fish friers, a baker and two confectioners, three tobacconists (one also a cycle dealer), four tailors, four drapers, two outfitters, a dressmaker, a milliner, four stationers (two were also printers), three boot and shoe dealers, a boot maker, a saddler, two jewellers (one also a watchmaker), three ironmongers, a tinsmith, three decorators (one also a plumber), a furniture dealer, five shopkeepers or general dealers, a hairdresser, and a chemist. There were also two banks, a post office and four public houses.

Architecturally and historically the High Street is one of the most interesting streets in Yorkshire but only a selection of the buildings can be mentioned here. Commencing at the east end on the

Milner's Yard behind 70 High Street. (*East Riding of Yorkshire Council*) In the later 19th century a good proportion of the population of High Street lived not on the street itself but in the yards at the rear. The long narrow back gardens or crofts, running to the North and South Back Lanes, were developed with terraced housing and workshops. In 1871 there were 100 houses in yards off the High Street accommodating 320 people. There were eight yards on the north side and eight on the south side. The most infamous and populous was the National School Yard which had 71 people living in a terrace of sixteen cottages.

High Street looking west 1949. (*East Riding of Yorkshire Council*) The first house on the right is 16, refronted in 1806 by William Stockell, attorney. The infamous Revd Cornelius Rickaby, curate of the Priory and master of the Grammar School, was a tenant in the mid-18th century. Nos 18-20 are late 17th century with moulded brick eaves cornice and band.

Edmunds, printers and newsagents, 45 High Street in 1947. *(Georgian Society for East Yorkshire)* As well as being William Kent's boyhood home it was owned for a time by Lewis Carroll's brother, Skeffington Lutwidge Dodgson. In the years 1864-93 the large front room on the first floor was the meeting room for the Local Board.

The Toft. A drawing by Francis Johnson showing a reconstruction of the front before the 1840s alterations. Note the ogee dome peeping over the roof.

north side with 16 High Street (Craven House). The charming three-bay, two-storey front with elegant doorcase dates from 1806, but, as with so many houses along the street, the interior reveals late 17th-century origins. The impressive façade of **22 High Street (The Dominican Convent)** was built in the 1850s by Dr Christopher Hutchinson, incorporating two properties. No. 29, a neat three-storey, three-bay house on the south side of the street was built around 1828 by Dr Humphry Sandwith, whose son Humphry became a national hero for his part in the siege of Kars during the Crimean War.

Nos. 39-41, a once-handsome Georgian build-ing was in part the Seven Stars Inn in the early 18th century and a century later the General Elliott Inn. The whole block had become a high-class draper's shop by 1828, firstly Wranghams then from 1878 Mainprizes.

Continuing along the south side The Toft, 43 High Street, was built by the wealthy merchant William Hudson in 1673, the year he was Chief Lord. Its orderly exterior of the 1840s contrasts with the flamboyant artisan-mannerist woodwork inside. The doorcases and chimneypieces are a riot of carved fruit, flowers and leaves in drops

and garlands. No two doorways are the same. The house has a splendid oak staircase that once ended in a glazed lantern with an ogee lead dome. The fine bow-windowed façade of 45 High Street similarly hides an interior with late 17th century woodwork, but it is more restrained as one would expect in a building of 1693. This is the house built by William Kent's father (see p.31).

34 High Street. *(Olga Reckitt)* It was the farmhouse of a small working farm of 40-50 acres in the 19th and early 20th centuries.

On the north side of the street 42-44 and 48 incorporate substantial chunks of stone from the priory, and 46 has charming bow-windows. 54 High Street is distinctively Victorian with its bold window surrounds and triangular pediments to the first floor. It was built around 1860 as the offices of the Bridlington Free Press.

Opposite, 47-49 High Street are on the site of the early 19th-century Cross Keys Inn, rebuilt 1860. By 1890 it was Foster Binnington's Drapery Ware-house. Next door Bestworth House, 51-53 High Street, was also once a draper's shop. Built c. 1712 by the collector of customs, Allan Lamont, it has an intriguing restored façade of seven bays with full-height pilasters irregularly spaced. Bought by the attorney John Grimston in 1733 it was tenanted by a succession of doctors until its purchase by a surgeon, Richard Kentish, in 1769.

Bestworth House, 51-53 High Street, 1986. *(Olga Reckitt)*

With the exception of the Manor House, 64 High Street, built 1785 for John Doeg, surgeon and man midwife, the remaining properties in the street are more commercial in character. The Board Inn, partly of c. 1700, was a superior grocery and wine merchant's from the late 18th century. No. 67, on the south side of the street, was Dales, ironmongers and agricultural implement makers from c. 1805 until the 1960s. The glazing bars of the unusual bay window are of brass and were made in the foundry that stood behind the shop. In 1871 Matthew Dale was employing sixteen men and five boys. Gordon Road was opened up on the south side of High Street in the 1890s and widened in 1964.

Returning to the north side the Globe Inn, together with 78-80 High Street, stands on the site of the Hustler mansion (see p.18), the largest house in the 17th century town. Here Henrietta Maria may have stayed in 1643. Later the house became the Black Lion Inn, renamed the Globe after 1782. It was rebuilt soon after 1833 by Thomas Cape as a grocer's shop and Post Office. Around 1907 82 High Street became the Globe Inn once again. On the west side of the Hustler mansion stood the medieval guildhall of the Guild of Our Lady which was dissolved in 1548. The site of the guildhall is now occupied by 92-96 High Street. In the 1850s-70s Edward Tindall, antiquarian, political activist and clay pipe maker, lived at the Old Guildhall, 92 High Street which was rebuilt by the saddler Ernest Cooper in the early 20th century.

Opposite is the Black Lion Inn that was kept by Henry Cook in the 1790s. It may be the same

64 High Street, 1947. *(East Riding of Yorkshire Council)* It has been known as the Manor House since 1990 when it became the offices of the Lords Feoffees and Assistants of the Manor of Bridlington.

Mid-19th century bill head for the Black Lion.*(Richard Marriott)*

building, described as lying near the Fish Shambles, which he fitted up as a Post Office in 1776. The inn had stabling for 40 horses and in the early 20th century, and probably long before, it was where the weekly corn market was held.

Market Place

The earliest reference to a market place in Bridlington is in a rental of 1545 that suggests that the market was then held near the priory. The regular shape of the present broad Market Place, in contrast to the rest of the Old Town, and its unusual position at the very edge of the settlement indicate that it was a late planned creation, probably of the mid-later 16th century, after the dissolution of the priory.

A survey of 1609 refers to the Market Place. It gives no clues to its location but this is likely to have been in its present position. In the years 1636-42 deeds describe a cottage on the south side as on 'Westgate in Market Place' and refer to nine cottages on the west side of the Market Place or Beast Market Place. The southernmost cottage was said to lie to the west of 'Bridlington Cross'. The cross, which had been replaced by buildings by 1740, stood on a slight rise at the southern end of the Market Place, known as Cross Hill. Whether it was just a cross on raised steps or a covered shelter of some kind is unknown.

Called variously the Beast Market Place in the 17th century and the Corn Market Place, or sometimes Swine Market Place, in the 18th century it was not favoured as a trading place. As John Thompson remarked in 1821 'the piercing blasts of the north' rendered 'the situation of the Market-place bleak and uncomfortable' and therefore the market, with moveable stalls selling 'butchers'-meat, vegetables, fruit and other necessaries' was chiefly held at the west end of the High Street. Butter, eggs, and poultry were sold from baskets on Cross Hill. Although a Corn Exchange was built in 1824, the farmers chose to trade their corn at the Black Lion Inn.

The principal buildings in the Market Place were inns, where the farmers gathered on market days to transact business. The inns in 1850 were the White Swan and the Nags Head on the east side and the Pack Horse, the Globe and the King's Head on the west side. The White Swan

The stocks and pillory on the west side of Market Place in the mid-19th century, drawn by William Fallowes. *(Lords Feoffees)* The stocks and pillory were in the Market Place by 1636. The artist, William Fallowes (1820-90), was a plumber, painter and glazier and lived at 34 Market Place.

Centre House, Market Place. *(Bayle Museum Trust)* Here public proclamations were made and election results declared. The buildings were demolished in 1913.

Coverley House, 23 Market Place c. 1880. *(Bayle Museum Trust).* One of the handsome late Georgian houses at the north end of Market Place. In the 1870s-80s it was a school for young ladies, day and boarding, kept by Miss Jennie Barmby, as principal and her sister Martha as housekeeper. In 1871 they had 17 boarders aged between 9-19, chiefly from Hull and the East Riding. The school closed c. 1900.

(now 32 Market Place), which had a club room and malt kiln in the 1790s, closed in the 1890s. No. 18 Market Place was known as the Ship Inn in the 1790s, the Tyger by 1805 and finally the King's Head in 1826. It closed in the early 1880s. Adjoining it to the south 17, now a veterinary surgery, was the Light Horseman by 1822. It was renamed the Globe in the 1840s and closed in the 1890s. Of the two surviving inns the Nags Head, rebuilt in the 1960s, is mentioned by name in 1723 and the Pack Horse in 1768.

The shops and trades of the Market Place were geared to the farming community. In 1901 there were two wheelwrights and agricultural implement makers (Thomas Robson and Son and Robert Watson), a saddler, a blacksmith and a veterinary surgeon. The early Old Town banks were also here. Hardings, the earliest Bridlington bank, was at 45 by 1823 and the Savings Bank, established 1837, was at 33 by 1850.

No. 1 Market Place had an interesting succession of uses. From c. 1780 to the 1870s it was Forths, the hatters. In the 1880s it became Hodgsons, gunmakers; and by 1913 (combined with 2) it was also a cycle agency, then by 1925 a motor engineers (Hodgson and Shields).

Corn Exchange, Market Place, c. 1970. *(Francis Johnson and Partners)* Originally built 1824 it was rebuilt on the same site in 1857 when it was given a Gothic stone façade. Rebuilt in 1972 as a house to the designs of Francis Johnson, for the Lords Feoffees.

Looking west along Westgate in the 1950s. *(Georgian Society for East Yorkshire)* The row of late 17th-century buildings from Hebblethwaite House to the Old Star Inn is followed by a three storey building of 1871. This was Wentworths, cabinet makers, house furnishers and undertakers. John Wentworth opened his shop in Westgate in 1849.

Westgate

Westgate once formed the main entry to Bridlington but with the building of the Well Lane bypass in 1973, it has become a quiet backwater. The east end of the street was largely commercial and the west end residential. Starting at the Market Place the first buildings are banks. Barclays on the north side was built in 1893 for the York Union Banking Company Limited and the HSBC bank (Midland) on the south side occupies one of Bridlington's most important buildings, Hebblethwaite House, 7-9 Westgate. Rebuilt in 1681 by the merchant Thomas Wilson it is a splendid example of a brick building in the artisan-mannerist style with original casement windows, a great rarity in the East Riding. It has contemporary woodwork inside including a fine oak staircase. It was purchased in 1762 by James Hebblethwaite (see p. 38); his son William added

Green Dragon Inn. *(Richard Marriott)* Bill head of 1844. Matthew Cranswick was the innkeeper 1834-54. The inn closed 1910 and all but part of the front wall was demolished.

the rainwater heads with the initials WH. The building became the York City and County Bank in July 1891. The Bridlington Rural District Council Offices were in Midland Bank Chambers until 1974.

Nos. 11-13 Westgate and the Old Star Inn are also of the late 17th century although much altered. The Star, first recorded by name in the 1790s, was called the North Star in 1802. The inn's earlier origins are clearly displayed in its front wall below the mock timber framing. The plinth and part of the surround of a blocked doorway are constructed of substantial stonework, almost certainly from the dissolved priory. Opposite the Star stood the Green Dragon, the town's principal inn through much of the 18th and early 19th centuries. It was the scene of vestry and manor court dinners and much official business was transacted there. In the 1760s it was the Post Office.

Further west the road widens and becomes purely residential. On the south side are three substantial houses. Firstly West End House,

The Avenue from the north. *(Hanover Property Management)* A handsome three-storey, five-bay front with angle pilasters and pilasters to the central bay. A typical Queen Anne house of the area. The rear has two elegant full-height bows. The Avenue was a boarding house for Bridlington School 1918-1931 and the Avenue Hospital from 1932 to the 1980s. It has now been successfully converted into retirement flats.

29 Westgate, which has its origins in a house built around 1720 for Jane Harrington, sister-in-law of the merchant Thomas Wilson, the builder of Hebblethwaite House. Internally it has many features of this date. In 1755 the house was bought by John Taylor, an attorney, who added rooms to the rear of the house c. 1760. Taylor, who was Chief Lord on seven occasions, was succeeded in the house, and firm, by his son Bryan Taylor, eight times Chief Lord, whose sister married the attorney Thomas Harland.

Westgate Lodge, 31 Westgate is another house once owned by the Taylors. Built by Sidney, son of Bryan Taylor, soon after 1828, it has many original internal features and an unusual decorative frieze to the central doorcase. Sidney Taylor, another lawyer, was clerk to the Lords Feoffees as well as being Chief Lord five times. Amongst other posts he was clerk to the Harbour Commissioners, and for 44 years clerk to the magistrates of the Dickering division. On Taylor's death in 1868 Westgate Lodge was purchased by the Thomas Prickett of The Avenue, next door, the grandest house in Bridlington.

The Avenue, dated 1714 on the rainwater heads, was built for the wealthy attorney John Grimston who also bought up properties opposite to lay out the grounds and plant the avenue that gave the house its name. In 1774 Grimston's great-nephew, Robert Grimston of Neswick Hall, sold the Avenue to the then tenant Marmaduke Prickett, yet another lawyer. The Pricketts, who became the town's leading family in the 19th century, added the porch and built the extensive stable block on the west side.

St John Street

St John Street was one of the medieval streets of Bridlington, but it has few surviving buildings from before the late 19th century. It was the route from the town to the harbour and no doubt took its name from St John of Bridlington. When first recorded in the 1530s it is called St John Gate, a name that is used interchangeably with St John Street from the 17th to early 19th centuries. In 1541 there were at least 48 cottages and three shops in the street and 138 households in 1851.

Amongst the heads of households in 1851 were sixteen agricultural labourers, ten shoemakers,

West End House by Francis Johnson *(with the permission of Mrs Brenda Dismore).* The distinctive façade with rusticated quoins and bold window surround (see also the house opposite) probably dates from its ownership 1869-1909 by Robert Medforth, corn miller and merchant. (see p. 75) Medforth was the first Mayor of Bridlington 1899-1900, Chief Lord 1904-5 and 33 years warden of the Priory Church.

The High School for Girls, St John Street, c. 1910. *(Christopher Ketchell)* Bridlington High School for Girls was opened in 1905 in the Elms. John Bilson's extension to the left is not shown. The Elms was built in the Tudor style in the 1850s for Dr Brett. This façade went in 1932 in one of a number of enlargements to the school.

Looking north up St John Street before it was widened. c.1905. *(Bayle Museum Trust)*

White Lodge, Quay Road c. 1900. *(Bayle Museum Trust)* Originally Rose Villa, built late 1830s for J.F. Lamplugh, soap manufacturer. Taken over by the Borough Council 1925. It was demolished for the new Town Hall.

nine tailors, five joiners, four bricklayers, two watchmakers, two tinsmiths, two blacksmiths and a whitesmith. There were a few shops including four butchers, two grocers, two general dealers and a confectioner, and three inns of which only the Ship Inn, so called by 1822, remains. The Scarborough Castle Inn, on the corner with Baylegate, was demolished in 1867 as the first stage in widening the street, which culminated in the wholesale demolition of the west side of the street largely in the years 1905-1914.

The buildings demolished included the Zion Congregational chapel, one of the four Nonconformist meeting places along the street by the 1830s. The others were the Quaker meeting house of c. 1700, a Methodist chapel of 1803 and the first Primitive Methodist chapel built 1833. Later replacements remain including the Primitive Methodist building of 1877, now a supermarket, the exotic Wesleyan chapel of 1884, now St John's Burlington Methodist Church, and the new Zion Congregational Church of 1906.

Quay Road

St John Street becomes Quay Road at Havelock Crescent. This section of the old route to the harbour was laid out in its present form and width at enclosure in 1771. There was hardly a building along the road before 1800, but by the early 1840s there was a sprinkling of villas, elegant terraces and Christ Church.

After the building of the railway station in 1846, at a point to satisfy the demands of the residents of both the Old Town and the Quay, the area north of the station at the junction between Quay Road and Station Avenue became considered as neutral ground. Known as the Gravel Pits it was renamed Midway Green in 1873 and nearby were built the Lloyd Hospital (1876), the police station and magistrates' court (1881), the Town Hall (1932) and Crown Buildings (c. 1970).

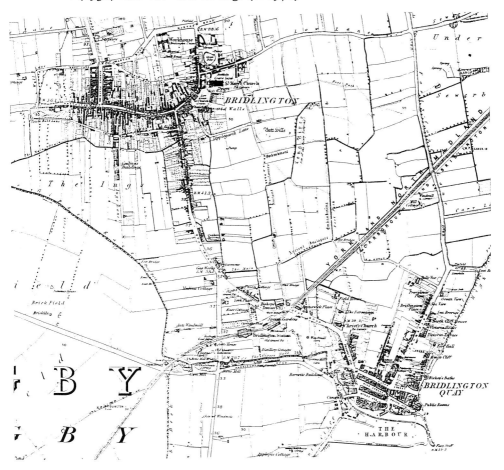

Bridlington and Bridlington Quay in 1850. Reduced from the 1st edition Ordnance Survey plan 6" to 1 mile, surveyed 1850, published 1854. The two settlements are still separate at this date although the Quay Road, noticeably wider than St John Street, is 'fringed with villa residences and private dwellings'.

Plan of the Quay

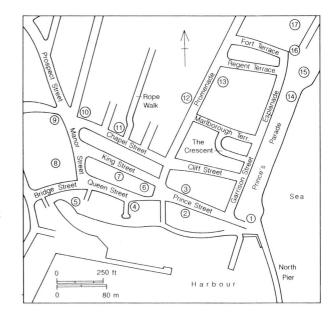

The Quay

From the 13th century to the early 16th century there are periodic references to the small settlement at the harbour as Castleburn. In 1534 a priory rental refers to cottages on 'the sea shore' as being 'by the See side otherwise Cast[l]eburne' but thirteen years before a resident considered himself as living at Bridlington Key when he made his will. Bridlington Key or just Key was the usual name for the settlement from the mid-16th century until the end of the 18th century. In the 1790s the modern form Quay was creeping in and by the 1820s had taken precedence.

In the 1530s the Quay was small. Rentals mention only nine cottages, 'beach houses', presumably store sheds on the edge of the sands, and 'herring houses'. A century later the Great Town Deed lists 32 houses and one shop at the Quay but by 1672 when the port was booming there were 120 houses. At this date the Quay consisted of little more than one street, the present Prince Street and King Street combined, some buildings westwards along the harbour top to Clough Hole and a few houses along the cliff between the North Pier and the fort. Further expansion was prevented by the common moor, which lay to the north and west, and the sea, to the south and east.

Limited development did take place because, by the terms of the Great Town Deed of 1636, the

Lords Feoffees undertook to grant land on the common for the erection of cottages to any whose cottage had decayed or fallen to ruin 'by reason of the wearing or washing away of the sea'. This requirement became redundant in 1771 when the commons were enclosed and the restrictions to the development of the Quay were lifted. Over the next 50 years the Quay grew from 'an inconsiderable village' to 'a neat lively and populous town'.

Erosion

Until the 1860s the topography of the Quay was constantly changing through coastal erosion and archaeological excavations are unlikely to reveal any vestige of a settlement on the coast from before the late middle ages. There are periodic records of the loss of land and buildings to the sea from the early 16th century to the mid-19th century. In 1819 a row of houses on the edge of the cliff was taken down though 'there had formerly been a street, with a carriage road, between it and the sea'. Concern increased when two 'elegant mansions' had to be taken down in 1834 and another was washed away in 1836.

There was some action by individual owners in building timber or brick sea walls to the north of the harbour but it was not until the Local Board became involved from 1866 onwards that the

Cottages on the edge of the cliff to the north of the harbour. Drawing by Fanny Waring 1805. *(F.F. Johnson)*

Site of New Spa and Gardens 1890. *(F.F. Johnson)*

protection became more permanent. However, the groynes that were built on the north side greatly increased the erosion to the south of the harbour in Hilderthorpe. Here the first attempt at building a sea wall in 1879 was a disaster and it was not until 1896 with the building of the Spa Wall that any effective protection was given.

Prince Street

Prince Street would have been the only street at the Quay in the 17th century. Until c. 1800 it was just called the Key street along with the present King Street. In the late 17th and early 18th centuries the street was lined with the new brick houses of the merchants and master mariners. In the confined area of the Quay the broad street provided them with the much needed space to store timber and other imports, an action that twice yearly brought them fines at the manor court for obstructing the highway.

Here lived the Rickabys, the Bowers and the Woolfes. The Rickabys had the grandest house; it stood on the north side of the street on a site now occupied by Newspot Newsagency and Pleasureland (3 and 4 Prince Street). Built c. 1710, probably for Giles Rickaby, the seven-bay three-storey mansion was similar in style to The Avenue, Westgate and Sewerby Hall. In 1851 it accommodated a household of 14, including the 61 year-old John Rickaby, his 26 year-old wife Louisa, three children, a housekeeper, a housemaid, a cook, a kitchen maid, a nurse, an under nurse, a male house servant, a coachman and a stable boy. Despite the increasing commercialisation of

Rickaby House. *(East Riding of Yorkshire Council)* Rickaby kept racehorses in a paddock on the east side of Promenade. The bow-windowed building on the right was the grocery and wine merchant's shop of James Stephenson.

Carriers' carts and the town bellman in Prince Street on market day, c. 1900. *(F.F.Johnson)* Note the changes to Rickaby House. On the far left is the New Inn before it was reduced in size on the widening of Cross Street in 1905. Marketing took place in Prince Street from the later 19th century until 1949.

Prince Street the Rickabys remained living there until the death of John Rickaby in 1860. Then its decline began. By the 1880s shop fronts had been inserted all across the front and bay windows added to the upper storeys on the right. In 1913 Southcotts, tailors, pushed an arcade through the centre of the building which in the 1920s became Shaw's arcade. The remnant of the Rickabys' house was rebuilt in the 1960s.

Prince Street was where visitors usually lodged in the early days of the resort. In 1796 John Courtney of Beverley took lodgings at 'Stephenson's the Grocers'. From the lodgings, which he liked 'very well', he could see the people dancing in the assembly rooms at the Ship Inn (27 Prince Street). The Ship, renamed the Britannia by 1812, had once been the house of the merchant John Bower. It was the chief inn at the Quay from the mid-18th century to the building of the Alexandra Hotel in 1866. The Britannia, largely rebuilt in the early Victorian period, was destroyed by enemy action in 1940 as was the Cock and Lion (25-26 Prince Street). Originally a 17th-century building with a celebrated oak-panelled room the Cock and Lion had been rebuilt in 1926-7.

George Hotel, Prince Street, 1927. *(East Riding of Yorkshire Council)* Until 1890 the road in front of the George was the 'Slipway' which sloped down to the North Pier.

Looking east along Prince Street. *(F.F.Johnson)* The Britannia Hotel with its rounded bays is on the right. Rebuilt in 1796 and much enlarged in the Victorian period it was said to retain Georgian features at the time of its destruction.

Looking west from the North Pier up the Slipway to Prince Street c. 1890. *(F.F. Johnson)* The Victoria Rooms adjoined the late 18th-century Cliff Terrace on the right of the picture.

Despite these losses the two oldest buildings in Prince Street are both inns; the New Inn, so called when it was taken over by the butler from Sledmere House in 1805, and the George Hotel (21 Prince Street). The latter was formerly the Tiger Inn and was not the original George Hotel, which was in King Street (see below). It is recorded as the Tiger Inn in 1822-58 and as the George Hotel in 1867.

Another inn, the Sheffield Arms, stood in the yard behind 16 Prince Street and was reached by the passages that still exist near the corner of Prince Street and Garrison Street. The inn had been known as the Newcastle Arms before the 1850s. The change of name probably reflects the Quay's change from being chiefly a port trading with the north-east to being a resort for South Yorkshire. The inn closed just before the First World War.

From the late 18th century onwards Prince Street increasingly became a commercial street. The merchants' houses, and eventually the lodging houses, gave way to a range of shops. In 1888 there were three chemists, three outfitters, three boot and shoe dealers, three grocers, two butchers, two confectioners, a jeweller, a tobacconist and a florist as well as two dining rooms. One of the confectioners was William Anfield, at 9, the founder of the firm famous for its cheesecakes. The principal shops were the grocers (Stephensons, Colleys and Coltharts), part of whose trade would have been supplying ships. Stephensons were grocers and wine merchants at 5 Prince Street for nearly 100 years from 1792. The shop became part of the Paragon Hotel in the 1890s and is now Brummels.

A number of the present businesses arrived between the wars. Woolworths was opened at 10-11 Prince Street in 1928, Marks and Spencer at 8 in 1932 and Notarianni's ice cream parlour at 15 in 1935. Woolworths, which had taken over 9 in 1937, and the neighbouring Foley's café, were bombed in 1940. On the south side John Bull's rock shop (19-20) was built for Ernest Hodgson in 1926. In the 1930s Premier Amusements were already at 22-23 Prince Street with Palladin Amusements next door. Macdonalds, 28, was built for Montagu Burton in 1932-3 on the site of a petrol station and car showroom opened 1919. It had been Grantham's refreshment rooms c. 1890-1905. Batchelor's draper's shop was in Commercial Buildings, the late 18th-century block facing eastwards down Prince Street, from the 1890s until recently.

King Street

King Street, so termed by 1806, was a new street laid out by the Lords Feoffees across Bridlington Moor in the late 17th century. It was here in the years 1660-1730 that the Lords granted plots on long leases to those who had lost houses and land to the sea. The plots varied in width east-west along the street but all were 24 yards (22 m.) in depth bounded to the north or south by the back streets, now known as Chapel Street and Queen Street.

Some of the plots were leased for 1000 years but others were held on shorter leases, and still are, including the site of the library. The early properties were a mixture of commercial and domestic. At the west end on the north side were malt kilns, warehouses and workshops in the early 18th century. The most westerly plot, acquired by a Manchester maltster in 1756, became the Victoria Brewery by 1850. The most easterly block on the south side was occupied by William Robinson,

J. STEPHENSON,
Bridlington Quay,
Dealer in Tea, Coffee, Chocolate, and Cocoa.
WITH EVERY OTHER ARTICLE IN THE

GROCERY LINE;
ALSO,
Confectionary, Sauces, & Pickles, Cask and Bottled London
PORTER,
STATIONARY, CHILDREN AND OTHER BOOKS,
Perfumery, with a great Variety of Fancy Articles.

The head of a handbill published by James Stephenson in 1806 on his return from a purchasing trip to London. In it he advertises a surprising range of exotic and unusual goods including: Westphalia hams, Gorgona anchovies for sandwiches, pickled India chillis, mangoes, curious Jamaican ginger, China oranges, preserved French apples, Italian 'vermacille', Turkey and Faro figs in boxes and small baskets, 'Sweppes Acidolous Soda Water', Brunswick Japan blacking for stoves, patent medicines, umbrellas, India carpeting and ornament shells, spectacle cases, Naples 'sope', gunpowder, prayer books and music paper.

Looking east along King Street c. 1890. *(F.F. Johnson)* Note the cobbled street and the elegant bowed fronts on the right, now replaced by the bank.

One of the original properties on King Street. *(F.F.Johnson)* With its distinctive shaped gable it is a typical building of the late 17th century. In the 1880s it and the adjoining building were replaced by a new shop for Schofields (now Cast and Martin 39-41 King Street).

master mariner, in 1773 when he obtained a licence to use his house (possibly 40) as the first Methodist Meeting House at the Quay.

The great width of the street at the west end encouraged its use for an unofficial market from the 1820s and as the resort developed from the 1860s King Street became Bridlington's commercial centre. The oldest continuous business is the King's Arms, which was an inn by 1824. Former inns in the street include the Ship Inn, at 35 King Street for a short time in the early 19th century, and the Sea Bird Inn at 51 King Street. Originally the Admiral Parker Inn, c. 1822-46, it was rebuilt as the Sea Bird in 1858.

The most substantial property in King Street was the house built c. 1792 by John Pitts (22-24). This five-bay three-storey brick house, with the centre three bays projecting under a pediment, had a handsome doorcase. Pitts, possibly driven out by the increasing commercialisation of the street, put the house up for sale in 1803. It was brought by Francis Fox, the landlord of the New Inn, and he opened it as the George Hotel in 1805. It closed c. 1832. From c. 1834 to 1863 the western half of the house was lived in by Arthur Strickland, a younger son of Sir William Strickland of Boynton, who had a museum there. He was chairman of the Harbour Commissioners. In

1870 the house was taken by Storrs, cabinet makers and house furnishers. They refronted the building in 1906 and pushed through the Royal Arcade. In 1938 it became a Hull Co-operative Society store. It is now Superdrug and retains an elegant Adam style plaster ceiling.

Hull Co-operative Society had already built 37 King Street, opposite, with its distinctive white faience façade, as a new drapery branch in 1913. It is on the site of a baker's shop kept successively by John Speck from the 1820s, William Anfield, of cheesecake fame, from 1847, and finally William Woodcock by 1858. The narrow lane on its east side was called Charity Lane or 'Speck's open' in the early 19th century.

Marks and Spencer had their first Bridlington shop at 34 King Street by 1921; it had previously been Rowntrees, grocers. Boots also had their first shop in the town when they took over Sharples, chemists (previously Mainprizes), at 23 adjoining Carltons department store. Carltons originated in the shop kept at 13 King Street by Chadwick and Slater, linen and woollen drapers, silk mercers, tailors, milliners and straw bonnet makers in 1857. Robert Carlton took over the *Bon Marché* store of Norman Jones in 1911 and extended the shop. Carlton's occupied 11-21 King Street when it closed in 1968. It was soon after replaced by the vast Binns store which was taken over by Boyes in 1998. To the west 5 King Street (Higginsons) was built on part of the site of the Victoria Brewery. Here was published the *Bridlington Quay Observer* 1857-99.

The number of banks is a sign of the street's commercial significance. The oldest established was the York City and County Bank (later the Midland Bank) at 14, rebuilt 1898. It closed in the 1930s and the building became the Borough Library in 1937. The library was extended in 1966 and 1973. Becketts Bank was at 6-8 (now Beauvais accountants) by 1905; note the BB on the doorcase. It became the Westminster Bank in 1923. In 1910 the National Provincial Bank was on the south-western corner of King Street and the London Joint City and Midland Bank on the north-western corner. The Savings Bank at 16-18 King St (now Lloyds TSB) was opened 1919 and Martins Bank opened a branch at 20 King Street in 1928 (now Scope).

John Pitts' house, 22-24 King Street. *(East Riding of Yorkshire Council)* Pitts was Lt-Colonel of the Bridlington Volunteer Artillery and Light Infantry during the Napoleonic Wars. He built Field House, 20 Victoria Road, c. 1806. It was then in open country.

Interior of Norman Jones and Company, *Au Bon Marché*, 1908. *(East Riding of Yorkshire Council)* Slater's drapery was taken over by Makins and Bean by 1888. Norman Jones came as manager; in 1897 he was a partner of Bean and by 1905 sole proprietor. On his death in 1911 *Bon Marché* became Carltons.

Many of the properties in King Street originally ran through to the North and South Back Streets, renamed Chapel Street and Queen Street in the early 19th century; some still do. These streets developed piecemeal.

Chapel Street

There was nothing but the common moor on the north side of Chapel Street until it was enclosed in 1771. Land adjoining the street was awarded in six plots, of one to five acres, and these were developed with workshops, corn warehouses and timber yards. The plots ran back a considerable distance and so provided an ideal siting for the long rope walk established behind 23-25 Chapel Street in 1789. The (Wesleyan) Methodist chapel, after which the street was named, was built in 1795, enlarged 1818-20 and rebuilt in 1873. The Primitive Methodists also built a chapel on the street, at the corner of North Street on the site of a large granary, in 1870. It was rebuilt on a grander scale in 1879. Closed in 1969 Iceland Foods now stands on its site.

Queen Street

The east end of Queen Street is particularly narrow, but after the Harbour Lites (23 Queen Street, the site of the Queen's House) it widens into a broad rectangle which was probably planned in the late 17th century when King Street was laid out. This helps support the view that the Queen's House stood at the western end of the Quay in 1643.

Some of the older looking houses at the Quay are on Queen Street, including 17-20 which look late 17th century, and the modest two-storey pantiled shops of the late 18th century. The chief building in the street was the Stirling Castle Inn, which was there by 1803. It was demolished in 1964 and replaced by the Ship Ahoy and adjoining buildings. The alleyway between 33 (Macfisheries) and 34 (Beside the Seaside Museum) leads to Garden Walk (also known as Garden Pales) which in 1871 was crammed with 22 cottages, those on the south side backing precariously onto the harbour, in which lived 20 mariners and 5 fishermen. Also off Queen Street on the south side is Queen's Square, where there is a good doorcase of c. 1800 and the alley known

Above: Quay Methodist Chapel, Chapel Street. *(Christopher Ketchell)* This impressive building designed by William Botterill of Hull, 1873, would be crammed with visitors for the services in the summer months. It closed in 2000.

Left: South side of Queen Street c. 1950. *(East Riding of Yorkshire Council).* The Stirling Castle has full height bows.

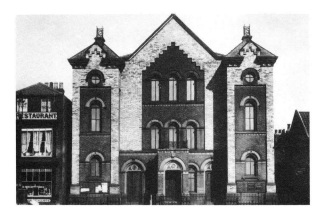

Primitive (Central) Methodist Chapel, Chapel Street. *(East Riding of Yorkshire Council)* Built 1879 to designs of William Freeman of Hull. It closed 1969 and soon afterwards was demolished.

as Ship Hill. There were two inns in the alley in the first half of the 19th century, the Star and yet another Ship Inn. There was also a 'bath saloon' from the 1860s. It was Gautier's Swimming Baths when it was destroyed in the Second World War.

Manor Street

Manor Street, 1871. *(F.F.Johnson)* The funeral procession for the victims of the 'Great Gale' lined up outside 6-10 Manor Street. On the right can be seen part of the house (now Barclays Bank) altered for Henry Boynton, c. 1820, when it was refronted with the large bows and portico.

Manor Street, known as New Buildings until the 1850s, was developed by the Lords Feoffees who still own most of the properties. In 1790-91 six lots on the west side of the street were assigned on 199-year leases and soon afterwards ten elegant Georgian houses, designed as lodging houses, were built. They included the Brunswick Hotel that has its origins in Frankish's Temperance Hotel established by 1846 and Barclays Bank. The latter was, like 7-8 and 9-10, a semi-detached pair with pedimented double doorcase in the

centre, but c. 1820 it was converted to one property for Henry Boynton who in 1832 succeeded to the baronetcy and the Burton Agnes estate. The buildings to the north of Barclays Bank were mostly rebuilt following bomb damage in the Second World War.

The Union Chapel shared by the Independents and Baptists was built c. 1817 on waste land at the north end of Manor Street. This was converted to the Manor House for the Rickaby family c. 1840. It was demolished 1928 for Lloyds Bank which was built on the site.

Prospect Street

Prospect Street was largely developed in the first decade of the 19th century. In 1800 five building lots were sold on the west side of the street, which was initially known as Spring Gardens. The land on the east side of the street was acquired about the same time by the builder and architect John Matson. Renowned as the builder, but not architect, of Flamborough lighthouse, Matson apparently sold the land off in lots for housing that he then designed and built. There were at least a dozen houses on Prospect Row, as the east side was known, by 1823. Matson lived there himself.

The street has been largely rebuilt and only 10-12 Wellington Road (formerly Prospect Row) retain their character. The original Half Moon Inn (10 Prospect Street) was built by 1806.

Promenade

Promenade was a new road laid out at enclosure in 1771, leading from the Quay across the former moor towards the Sewerby road. Originally called Cliff Road it was renamed Promenade sometime between 1813 and 1823 when the road began to develop. Amongst the earliest properties were villas and select lodging houses, such as North Cliff House and Sea Breezes, on the east side to the north of the later Fort Terrace. By 1850 the west side was lined with elegant terraces as far as the present Tennyson Avenue. Of these only the delightful Belle Vue Terrace c. 1840-2 survives, still with open grounds in front. Elsewhere there are odd remnants of the late Georgian and early Victorian development including the late 18th-century doorcase to 17 Promenade and the first floor bow at 43 Promenade.

Richard Allen & Co, Promenade, c. 1900. A drawing by F.S. Smith of Hull. Richard Allen, draper and silk mercer opened his store at Bridlington in 1874. On three floors with a lift the shop employed fifty staff. It closed on 1 January 1977 and was demolished soon afterwards.

Promenade looking north c. 1895. *(F.F. Johnson)* In the far distance can be seen the spire of Holy Trinity church, and in the middle distance the turret of the Congregational church on the right and the pediment of the United Methodist Free Church on the left. Note also the single-storey Cheapside with its row of wooden gables.

The southern part of the street, as with all the older parts of the Quay, had taken on a commercial rather than domestic character by the 1880s with the usual array of drapers, grocers, butchers, and chemists as well as a brewery. On the east side, to the north of Marlborough Terrace, was a row of 'temporary' wooden shops known as Cheapside erected in 1869. The premier stores were those of the grocer Charles Crannis and the draper Richard Allen. Ernest Whiteley opened his first shop at 65 Promenade in 1901, moving to the present location (67) in 1906.

The places to visit on Promenade were the two chapels, Rowntree and Taylor's café, and the three 'pleasure palaces', the Winter Gardens opened 1922, the Lounge opened 1928 and the Regal Cinema opened 1938.

Esplanade

This street, referred to without the definite article, takes its name from The Esplanade laid out in 1828 on the site of the fort. The present street runs from Cliff Street to Regent Terrace. Confronted by the garish façades, lights and noise of the amusement arcades that now line Esplanade it is hard to imagine that it was once the location of some of the most select lodging houses and private villas at the Quay. Above the arcade fronts

the upper storeys of some of the predecessor buildings can still be seen.

Esplanade was developed in the 1820s-30s, firstly with a group of five houses at the northern end (1-5), then from the southern end with the first Primitive Methodist chapel at the Quay built 1833, the site of which is now occupied by 11-12 Esplanade (an amusement arcade). North of the chapel, set back and almost backing onto Promenade was Poplar, later Bay View, Cottage with a long walled garden running down to Esplanade. Then came the large Sandon House, 9 Esplanade, with a walled front garden, and finally a terrace of three houses (6-8 Esplanade) with modest front gardens

It was in the 1890s that the character of the street began to change, well evidenced by the fate of Sandon House. In 1897 Fields, grocers of Hull, acquired Sandon House. Soon afterwards they built the Oriental Café on the front garden, to the designs of Smith and Brodrick of Hull. Behind was laid out the 'Garden of a Thousand Lights' which was covered by cast-iron and glass in 1901 to become the Winter Gardens. This was converted into a skating rink in 1909, then to a concert hall in 1911, and films were being shown there in 1912. In 1928 it became the Esplanade Café and Lounge Theatre.

Esplanade looking south 1928-9. *(Christopher Ketchell)* The half-timbered gable end to The Lounge and the large semi-circular window and second-floor bows on the adjoining Electric Rock Factory, recently built for W. Askham of 'Askham for Rock' fame, are still visible today.

Field's Oriental Café, 9 Esplanade c. 1900. *(Norman Creaser)* It was built on the front garden of a seafront villa, Sandon House, the roof of which can just be glimpsed behind the café.

The harbour: an outline history

The extent and nature of the harbour in the middle ages is unknown although it seems that there were two piers. A north and south pier are mentioned in the early 16th century. It has been calculated that the north pier, more correctly the east pier, was about 190 feet (58 m.) in length and the south pier at least 60 feet (18 m.) in 1580. It is probable that the harbour was then of much the same extent as it was in the late 18th century and that the Elizabethan north pier lay to the east of the present North Pier, with the Elizabethan south pier following a line a little to the north of the present Chicken Run Jetty. The harbour would have covered some 5 acres (2 ha.). The piers consisted of wooden compartments infilled with stone.

Extensive repairs were carried out in the late 1530s using stone from the demolished Priory buildings, but storm damage and the constant erosion of the coastline meant that the harbour was often said to be 'in decay' from the mid-16th to the late 17th centuries. The task was too great for the Lords Feoffees and the income from the pier rates was too little, to carry out a major rebuilding. In 1697 an Act of Parliament was obtained whereby fifteen local gentry and the Wardens of Trinity House at Hull were appointed to oversee the maintenance of the piers. These men, known variously as the Trustees or Commissioners for Bridlington Piers, were to receive a passing toll collected from the north-east colliers and

The harbour and piers.

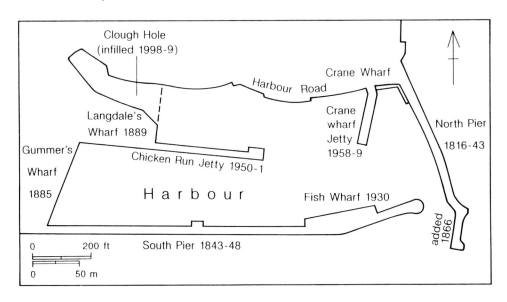

carry out the repairs to the harbour. The Pier
Commissioners appointed by the 1697 Act took
over the maintenance of the harbour from the
Lords Feoffees of the Manor of Bridlington. The
Lords Feoffees continued to collect an annual
pier rate that they passed to the Commissioners.

Both piers were completely rebuilt in the early
18th century and the South Pier was rebuilt on
new foundations 1719-55. The advice of the leading civil engineer John Smeaton was sought in
1778, and again in 1791, but no immediate action
was taken. Eventually in 1801-5 a 60 foot (18 m.)
extension of the North Pier was completed and
cased in stone on the seaward side. In the following three years a further 180 feet (55 m.) of the
North Pier was encased in stone. Deterioration
continued and the engineer John Rennie drew up
proposals in 1816 for an 'entire New Harbour'
that was rejected in favour of a scheme proposed
the year before by the lesser known Simon Good-
rick. The latter's plan was largely followed to produce the present harbour.

A new North Pier was built to the west of the old
pier. It was begun in or soon after 1816 but was not
finished until 1843; it was 608 feet (185 m.) long,

Bridlington harbour from the air
looking east, 11 November 1953.
(Yorkshire Post)

nearly 100 feet (31 m.) longer than the old pier. A further 120 feet (37 m.) was added in 1866 when it reached its present extent. In the years 1843-8 a new South Pier was built to the plans of James Walker. It was constructed in a more southerly position and the area of the harbour was increased from 5½ acres (2.2 ha.) to 12 acres (4.9 ha.). The new pier was 1,500 feet (458 m.) long compared with the 1,100 feet (336 m.) of the old pier. It is a remarkable testimony to the skill of the civil engineers and builders that these piers, despite continual battering by the seas, stand today virtually as built over 150 years ago.

'An Act for improving the Piers and Harbour of Bridlington ... and for rendering the same more safe and commodious as a Harbour of Refuge' passed in 1837 had broadened the representation of the Commissioners of the Piers and Harbour of Bridlington to include seven representatives of the Lords Feoffees of the Manor of Bridlington as well as East Riding gentry and clergy. It is on the basis of this 1837 act and a confirmation act of 1928 that the Harbour Commissioners still care for the piers and harbour today.

Sources

A fuller list of sources will be given in the longer work D. Neave, *Port, Resort and Market Town: A history of Bridlington,* to be published at the end of 2000.

The principal printed sources are:

K.J. Allison 'Bridlington' in *Victoria County History East Riding* vol. 2 (1974) pp. 29-106

M.E. Ingram *The Manor of Bridlington and its Lords Feoffees* (1977)

J.S. Purvis *Bridlington Charters, Court Rolls and Papers* (1926)

J. Thompson *Historical sketches of Bridlington* (1821)

Other printed sources include:

Jean Boudriot *John Paul Jones and the Bonhomme Richard* (1987)

J. Earnshaw *A Reconstruction of Bridlington Priory* (1975)

W.T. Lancaster *Abstracts of the Charters and other documents contained in the Chartulary of the Priory of Bridlington* (1912)

M.J.A. Mortimore *Bridlington School: A History* (1999)

Susan and David Neave 'The early life of William Kent' *Georgian Group Journal* 6 (1996) pp. 4-11

M. Prickett *An historical and architectural description of the Priory Church of Bridlington* (1831)

J.S. Purvis *St John of Bridlington* (1924)

F.A. Slim and H.L. Gee *Bridlington 1899-1949* (1949)

I. and M. Sumner *Bridlington (Britain in Old Photographs)* (1995)

M. Wilson *Any more for sailing? A personal look at Bridlington Harbour* (1996)

Trade and street directories 1798-1939 and guides to Bridlington 1805-1999

Newspapers: *Bridlington Chronicle, Bridlington Free Press, Hull Advertiser* and *York Courant.* Also 'Annals of Bridlington' cuttings from local newspapers compiled by W. Taylor and A.E. Matthewman, 59 volumes, 1867-1942 in the Local Studies Collection, Bridlington Library. There is a wealth of printed ephemera and photographs and other illustrations in this collection.

Unpublished sources:

K.L. Mayoh 'Comparative Study of the Resorts on the Coast of Holderness' M.A. thesis, University of Hull, 1961

E. Mellor, typescripts on numerous topics in Bridlington Library.

Principal documentary sources:

Lords Feoffees' Records, Town Chest, Bayle, Bridlington: Manorial records and leases.

East Riding of Yorkshire Archives and Records Service, Beverley: Bridlington deeds 1708-1820; Quarter Sessions records; Bridlington Priory Church records; Nonconformist registers; Bridlington enclosure award and plan;

Harbour Commissioners' records; Bridlington Corporation records including building plans 1878-1939 and Bridlington shipping registers 1786-1847.

Hull University Archives, Brynmor Jones Library, University of Hull: Lloyd-Greame of Sewerby and other estate collections; Diaries of John Courtney 1788-1805.

Borthwick Institute of Historical Research, University of York: Wills 1500-1730 and inventories 1688-1730; Cause papers and visitation records.

Public Record Office, Kew: Port books for Hull (including Bridlington); Customs and Excise records.

Acknowledgements

First and foremost we would like to acknowledge the help of Sydney Thompson who put his great knowledge of Bridlington's history at our disposal and who most willingly read through the text of this book. Other long-standing Bridlington friends who contributed in various ways include Charles Brear and Barbara Walker and the late Francis Johnson, Edward Ingram and Olga Reckitt.

Much of our research was carried out in local libraries and record offices and we would especially like to thank Nicola Bayley, former reference librarian and the other staff at Bridlington Reference Library; Pamela Martin, Jennifer Stanley and staff of Beverley Reference Library; the staff at Hull Local History Library and Hull City Record Office; Keith Holt, Ian Mason, Carol Boddington, Dr Mike Rogers and Helen Clark and other staff of the East Riding of Yorkshire Archives and Records Service; Brian Dyson and the staff of the University Archives, Brynmor Jones Library, University of Hull and Professor David Smith and staff at the Borthwick Institute of Historical Research, University of York. Thanks are also due to Nial Adams of the East Yorkshire Museums Service, Martin Foley and other staff at Sewerby Hall and Mike Cawthorn and Rob Tranmer of East Riding of Yorkshire Council. Assistance and information was willingly provided by Bernard Langton, David Mooney, Robin Sharpe, Clive Wilson and the Bayle Museum Trust; by Barry Gray, chairman, and the staff of the Harbour Commissioners; and by Chris Ketchell who was, as always, generous in his loan of material.

Amongst others who have kindly provided information or illustrations we wish to thank the following: Ann Blanchard; C.M. Burton; Dr Wendy Childs; Lance Cook; Martin Craven; Norman and June Creaser; Brenda Dismore; John Earnshaw; the late Bernard Foster; R. Hartley; M. Holland; the late Joan Horspool; Robin Horspool; Professor Bernard Jennings; Richard Marriott; Malcolm McKie; Neil Newby; Mike Oakenfull; Eric Palmer; Leslie Powell; Brian Rodgers; Elsie Thompson; Deborah Turnbull; Richard Walgate; Mike Wilson; Dr Terence Wilson; Dennis Whitehead; Professor Donald Woodward and all those who responded so willingly to our newspaper appeal for reminiscences of Bridlington holidays or provided information for the Beside the Seaside museum.

We would like to thank Mike Godwin, Head of Libraries and Community Services, East Riding of Yorkshire Council for his support and for giving permission to reproduce photographs from Bridlington Library and also John Spencer and Hull University Photographic Service for copying these and other illustrations belonging to the Lords Feoffees and the Bayle Museum Trust. The maps were expertly drawn by Mike Frankland and the reconstruction of Bridlington Priory by Les Turner, based with permission on the work of John Earnshaw.

Permission to reproduce illustrations was given by the Bayle Museum Trust; British Library; British Museum; Bodleian Library, University of Oxford; Cambridge University Collection of Air Photographs; the Trustees of the Chatsworth Settlement; Georgian Society for East Yorkshire; Hanover Property Management; Lord Henniker; Sir Tatton Sykes Bt.; Department of Archaeology, University of York and the Yorkshire Post.

Finally we would like to thank the Lords Feoffees and Assistants of the Manor of Bridlington for commissioning the research and writing of this history and their interest, and patience, throughout the project. We are most grateful for the support of Sally Bell, Administrator to the Lords Feoffees, who has greatly eased our task and to Sandra Church and Colin Barrass.

Index of Buildings, Streets and Places (*Bridlington only*)

Bridlington or Burlington?

The variation Berlinton, of the name of the town, occurs in a 12th-century charter but Burlington is not in common use until the 17th century. Although in official documents Bridlington was still invariably used in the 17th and 18th centuries, the choice of the title Earl of Burlington by Richard Boyle, 2nd Earl of Cork, for his English peerage in 1665 suggests this had become the preferred spelling and pronunciation by this date. It was the use of Burlington as the Boyle family title which has given the name world wide prominence. The *Burlington Magazine* and the music hall song 'Burlington Bertie' take their name from Burlington House, formerly the London seat of the Boyles (now home to the Royal Academy) and the nearby Burlington Arcade, and not from the Yorkshire town.

It was almost certainly the coming of the railway in 1846 and the use of Bridlington for the station name that led to the abandonment of Burlington. A copy of the *Burlington Reporter* newspaper in 1848 has only two uses of the name Burlington in reports or advertisements and 27 uses of Bridlington or Bridlington Quay.